HIGHWAY 35

HIGHWAY 35

Travels around East Cape

Text by JOHN WOODS

Photographs by PETER QUINN

Foreword by Witi Ihimaera

REED

NEW ZEALAND GEOGRAPHIC

'This'll probably be young Luke's first and last taste of the drover's life,' says Ron Brown as he and his sidekick Luke Abbot herd cattle along Highway 35 near Opotiki. Mobs of up to 500 cattle used to be common on the Coast as drovers, averaging 6-7 km a day and renting night paddocks from farmers along the way, took stock to Waikato and South Auckland for slaughtering. The practice may soon be outlawed as traffic counts rise and the number of logging trucks increases. But with an estimated 350,000 cattle (and 2.5 million sheep), the region still enjoys the reputation of having the highest intensity of beef cattle in the country.

At Rongomaitapui, the wharenui (meeting house) of Hinerupe Marae at Te Araroa, the Apostolic pastor's wife Chris Baker takes a back seat to look after her grandchildren while husband Arthur exhorts the congregation to 'open your homes, open your lives, share what you've got with one another.' The Christian message has been preached here since 1840, when Bishop William Williams brought Anglicanism to the Coast.

Just 6 km and what seems a light year away from the highway lies Waipiro Bay, with a population of 99 at the last census. Before the inland road became good enough for cars and bypassed it in the 1920s, Waipiro Bay was a bustling port, staging post, county administration centre and hospital base. Today its old shipping offices are empty ruins, and Sir Robert Kerridge's first movie theatre serves as the dining hall of the local marae. This child's family owns the peace and quiet of the derelict general store, beside a churchyard where the sheep are seldom of the human kind.

Shearers Robin Chaffey and Rob McKenzie (wiping face) take a break to oil their handpieces during a winter shear on Opiki Station near Te Puia Springs.

'Ngati' horses and cowboys Nig Manuel and Rapata Kaa revel in the open spaces of the East Cape, where horses have long been a vital means of transport and a part of the way of life. During the First World War a contingent of Ruatoria soldiers earned a reputation as outstanding members of the Mounted Rifles troops at the war zone. In the Second World War Ngati Porou soldiers in the Maori Battalion were fondly known as 'the cowboys'.

Overleaf: The Cape—mainland New Zealand's eastern extremity—remains wild and rugged beneath torrid skies and surging seas. Two kilometres offshore, East Island is a landmark with a legacy of shipwrecks and drownings. Thirteen ships sank there prior to 1906 when a lighthouse was installed. Landslides and difficulties with landing supplies forced the relocation of the light to the mainland in 1922.

13

'Poor as can be, but living the lives of kings'—a Coastie's description of the laid-back lifestyle on New Zealand's easternmost seaboard—means there's always time for loving and laughing. Father and daughter Wallace and Jardine Walker make that quintessential East Coast connection while whanau and friends fish from Hicks Bay wharf for kai moana to put on the table tonight. Hicks Bay is one of a few dozen isolated communities on the Coast.

Published by Reed Books, a division of Reed Publishing (NZ) Ltd, 39 Rawene Rd, Birkenhead, Auckland.
Associated companies, branches and representatives throughout the world.

ISBN 0 7900 0520 4

Editors: Kennedy Warne, Peter Dowling
Design: Kennedy Warne
Map by *New Zealand Geographic*/Glenn Conroy Creative

First published 1998

Jacket photograph: Nig Manuel and Rapata Kaa, sunrise, East Cape.
Half-title page photograph: Adrian Sutherland, Apostolic biker along Highway 35.
Back jacket photograph: Father and daughter Wallace and Jadine Walker, Hicks Bay Wharf.

Printed in Hong Kong

For our children, who know and love this place too:
Reuben, Coby, Israel, Sama and Buck Woods.
Aroha and Mariah Quinn, and their little brother Daniel
whose memory lives on with these photographs.

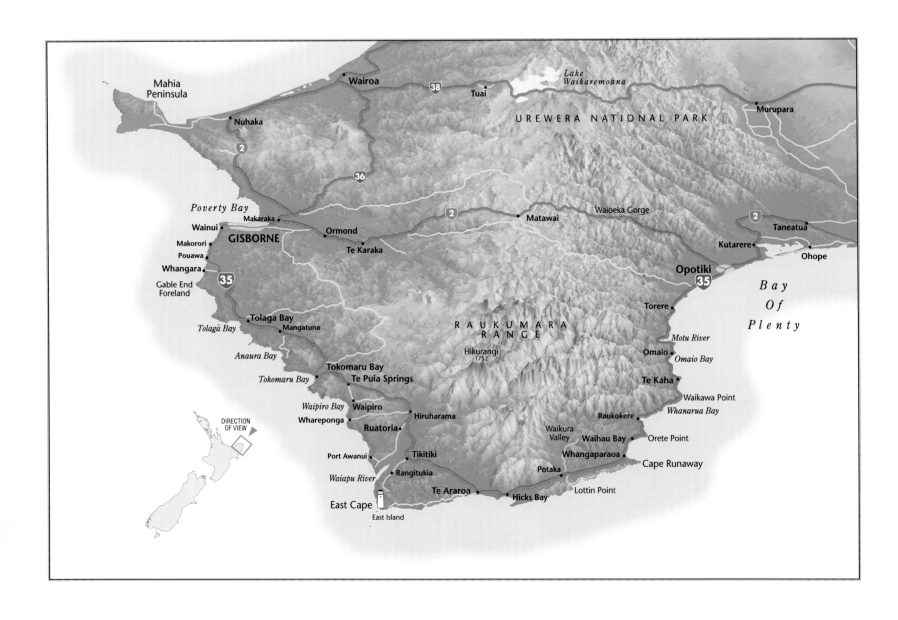

Mahia
Peninsula

Wairoa

Lake
Waikaremoana

Tuai

UREWERA NATIONAL PARK

Murupara

Nuhaka

2

36

Poverty Bay

Makaraka

Wainui

Ormond

2

Matawai

Waioeka Gorge

2

Taneatua

Makorori

GISBORNE

Te Karaka

Kutarere

Ohope

Pouawa

Whangara

Opotiki

35

Gable End
Foreland

35

*Bay
Of
Plenty*

Torere

Tolaga Bay

Tolaga Bay

Mangatuna

RAUKUMARA
RANGE

Motu River

Omaio

Omaio Bay

Anaura Bay

Hikurangi
1752

Te Kaha

Tokomaru Bay

Tokomaru Bay

Te Puia Springs

Waikawa Point

Whanarua Bay

DIRECTION
OF VIEW

Waipiro Bay

Waipiro

Raukokere

Whareponga

Hiruharama

Waikura
Valley

Waihau Bay

Ruatoria

Orete Point

Port Awanui

Tikitiki

Whangaparaoa

Cape Runaway

Waiapu River

Rangitukia

Potaka

Lottin Point

Te Araroa

Hicks Bay

East Cape

East Island

CONTENTS

FOREWORD

If our heart was a country, this would be the road running through the middle of it.

I RECKON I WAS born on the side of Highway 35.

All my life I've had the sky above, the earth below, and that road stretching way back into my past and way ahead into the future. It wasn't milk that I was weaned on either; before the road was tar-sealed, half the dust I've ever eaten came from that highway.

Like all the people on the East Cape, I've come to think of Highway 35 not just as a road but as a way of life, and this marvellous book shows why. For some people the road might be a way of getting from one place to the next, but for us it connects all the home places like Makaraka, Gisborne, Wainui, Whangara, Tolaga, Toko, Tikitiki, Ruatoria, Hicks Bay right around to Opotiki and makes us all Coasties. God might have created Adam and Eve, but his very special creation was the Coastie man and woman, whom he set down in their own Garden of Eden, right next to Mount Hikurangi.

There have been times when we've loved the East Cape and other times when we've sworn at it. On the plus side, you can keep your *Baywatch* beaches; the beaches past Whangara are to die for, and they get better the further around the Cape you go. On the debit side, that land and people can be sorely challenging, with drought in summer and storms in winter testing everyone to the limit. Hard land breeds hard people. Life has not always been easy, jobs are sometimes hard to find, but, hey, the people are still among the most decent and fair I've known. Yes, we've had our troubles, but we've also had our triumphs. And we're stubborn as.

Highway 35 can be the fastest road in the universe when you're not in a hurry and the slowest when you are. It's the road that links us with our history. Our fore-bears came up that road to settle the land. Our families saw their sons and daughters go down that road to wars on the other side of the world. Today, we continue to travel that road as farmers moving stock, locals going to weddings and engagement parties, kids travelling to school, parents travelling to stock sales or the races, young sportsmen and women playing against each other in rugby, hockey and basketball games.

We've loved and laughed on that road. Sometimes, we've gotten into a tie and suit and cried, too, when we've had to farewell one of us on his or her way back up that road, going home to be buried.

All this is why, if our heart was a country, there's no doubt that Highway 35 would run right through the middle of it. So this book is a special pleasure because it is about the road that has run through all of our lives.

Peter Quinn's photographs show us as we are; you don't get dirtier than us, but we can also scrub up pretty well too. And John Woods' text truly shows that he could take the title of the Mad Max of East Cape. He is a true defender of the highway.

For those of you who live in Gisborne and on the East Cape, I'm sure you will see your own stories here. For those who don't, this book will show just how much you're missing—and the special welcome you'll find when you do visit.

As for me, my memories of Highway 35 include sleeping in my dad's car or beside the road at night. The stars were wheeling overhead and I was not, ahem, always alone, so I guess you could also say that I've had a lot of my education on that road, some of it more from the School of Life syllabus than Tolaga Bay Primary. Californians may sing 'Get your kicks on Route 66,' but as far as I'm concerned, 'If you want to feel truly alive, try Highway 35.' Oh yes, and I was always good at dragging off the traffic cop who used to wait at the Makarori turnoff.

New Zealand heartland?

You can look all your life, but I reckon you'll never come closer to it than this.

Witi Ihimaera

1

IT WAS THE KIND OF East Coast day when summer looks set to stretch out for the whole year. Sri Lanka was thrashing the New Zealand cricket team on TV, but no one in the public bar could care less. The publicans, Elliott and Helen Grace, were reading the paper and licking ice-creams, relaxing before the start of afternoon trade at their 1920s Makaraka pub on the outskirts of Gisborne. I was there for a quick ceremonial beer before starting out on Highway 35. The only other patron, a regular, was lingering over his daily noggin.

The paper had a front-page article on this season's 'Operation Jane'. Police had recovered and destroyed $25 million worth of cannabis plants on the Coast, it said.

'They'll be watching you,' said Helen from her perch on a bar stool. 'The older Coasties are pretty good—they'll take you at face value. But some of the younger ones are very suspicious. They'll think you're undercover, unless you can prove otherwise.'

I stepped outside into the blue haze and asphalt shimmer and took a long look down the straight towards Gisborne. Doubtless such a day inspired Gisborne's Civic 30,000 Club in 1946—when the population stood at 17,000—to launch its subsequently successful population drive with a 44-page picture-book bearing the effusive title, 'Come to Sunny Gisborne on sea—the California of New Zealand—Orchard and Vineyard of the South Seas.'

Highway 35 bolts through the main street of Gisborne—Gladstone Road— as if eager to get to the bucolic Coast that lies ahead. This set of traffic lights is one of just two on the entire highway, both in Gisborne. The model ship on a pole is a reminder that Captain James Cook made his first New Zealand landfall on the nearby beach in 1769.

So it begins. State Highway 35, the main provincial artery running 334 km from Makaraka up and around East Cape to Opotiki. Slow, narrow, bumpy, meandering, magnificent.

I'm driving an inconspicuous Rent-A-Wreck Ford Laser with surfboard

and fishing rod on top, and bottles of wine and square gin in the boot—koha for my hosts, whoever they will be. Gifts are the only passport I'll need on this road.

Like most people who travel with solitude in the passenger seat, I also bring a cargo of memories and wistfulness. I've travelled this road for 35 years. First as a kid on a family tenting holiday, when long stretches were still gravel. Later I delivered beer on it, when my parents ran a pub in Opotiki. I rode it in my student holidays as a labourer on the back of hay trucks and on a double-decker cream truck, collecting the grey iron cans from tiny dairy farms that are long gone.

I've toured it and raced on it by bicycle. I've even worn a Jewish prayer cap and made sacrificial offerings on it—if that's what you can call the delinquent action of cliff-dropping a friend's Humber 80 to a watery grave more than a hundred feet below the highway. As eighteen-year-old school-leavers departing the Coast for the Big Smoke (Auckland, Wellington and beyond), five of us had met on Maraenui Hill, 40 km from Opotiki, to salute the sad end of a great summer and—something I

realised only later—the end of boyhood.

Now I live on 35. Until 1990, when the Ministry of Works put in a 1.8-km bypass to cut out our village, the highway ran past the gate of my oceanfront home at Wainui Beach, where the full coastal splendour of the road is first en-countered heading north from Gisborne. And I drive 35 all the time—in pursuit of surf, fish, adventure, friends and escape.

I will open by showing my hand: I love it here. The way the rising sun creeps out of an empty sea. The heat and the remoteness of a place that contains

The welcoming river entrance to Turanganui, the Maori name for Gisborne, is
a thoroughfare for fishing boats, kayaks, canoes and pleasure craft taking
advantage of the sunny days and alluring seas that abound in the place
Captain Cook inappropriately named Poverty Bay.
Opposite page: Rivers converge in downtown Gisborne, where a once thriving
port now provides shelter for the local fishing fleet and wharfage for one or two
ships at a time. The city of Gisborne is pictured from Kaiti Hill, once a
strategic fortress and lookout.

Reads Quay, named after the merchant who founded Gisborne and who once employed the infamous Maori leader Te Kooti Rikirangi, still seems like a colonial town of yesteryear thanks to civic pride in the old architecture, and not a lot of pressure for progress.

10 percent of the North Island's land mass yet less than 1 percent of its population. I love its secrets—the secrets of Maori history and folklore, of fishing and hunting grounds, of the poor and the blessed. I love the inevitable mixing of cultures, which makes it a home for the improbable and the unexpected. I love the fact that the Coast—for most New Zealanders a distant hinterland—is for the people who live here a place apart, with an identity and meaning all its own. And I love the fact that a shadow reality haunts and mythicises the Coast.

On 35 you travel the least-travelled regional roadway in New Zealand into the part of the country least visited by international tourists—18,000 is the last official figure from the New Zealand Tourism Board. Locals don't mind the statistic at all. Near East Cape, roadmen joke that their vehicles make up most of the daily traffic, though radiata logging trucks are changing that. On a carriageway seldom wider than a minimum two-lane road, these juggernauts have become the modern-day curse of the Coast.

On 35 you're wise to slow down and stay slowed down. You might turn a corner and find yourself among wandering cows or horses, or come across a sunburned farmer shooing sheep across the road, or pass a kid on a bike with a pet pig trotting along behind. Ninety percent of the cars are clapped-out V8s and Big Sixes: Holdens and Falcons and Valiants in the nothing-to-$5000 price bracket. They chug about like ghosts on an abandoned stage set, and everywhere the roadsides and fields are decorated by their wrecked remains. 'Statues', locals call them. Periodically, the police hold amnesty days, when unlicensed drivers come forward in their unregistered, unwarranted vehicles to sit tests and get legal. One such amnesty yielded a third of the community's adult population.

MAKARAKA CROSSROADS, the start of my pilgrimage. Roseland Tavern. Makaraka Dairy ('Your Happy One-Stop Shop'). Makaraka Butchery ('No Bum Steers Here'). A few old colonial cottages, a fish and chip shop, a saddlery, a gas station.

Highway 35 heads straight in and out of Gisborne city, through the main street where you can still get a three-course roast meal at The Mill tearooms for under ten bucks. U-turning motorists and shoppers in shorts, singlets and bare feet tell you there's no hurry around here. The phrase 'rush hour' is not in common currency.

It's been this way for the 118 years since the town was founded as a trading port. Soon the highway is to be re-routed around the seaward perimeter to cut out the Gladstone Road thoroughfare, where a multimillion-dollar mall development is proposed to jazz up the main street shopping area in time for Year 2000 celebrations. But cosmetics won't change the fact that in its back streets Gisborne is a placid, small-town world of village greens, riverside vistas and corner dairies: an

Shifts run round the clock seven days a week when the squash season is on, shiploads of the vegetables being exported fresh to Japan. Some squash is made into powder for export as an ingredient in soup mixes. Organically grown product fetches a premium on the world market, and promises to generate more jobs and export income for the region.

Smash Palace, a zany bar and winery in one of Gisborne's industrial areas, is a popular back-street venue for after-work drinkers and out-of-town visitors alike. Proprietor Phil Parker runs his boutique winery out the back, surrounded by wrecks of Morris Minors and a DC3 aeroplane. Pop art, sculpture and a convivial atmosphere have earned it a popular place in the social culture of the East Coast.

oasis of sunlit optimism suspended in a sleepy haze of laissez-faire conservatism.

Gisborne's 30,000 residents are cloistered in a tight-knit community that is isolated from New Zealand's main routes by tough drives through winding gorges: three hours south to Napier, two hours to Opotiki (via the direct route on Highway 2), seven hours to both Auckland and Wellington. Commercially, the city is a general factotum with one of everything. It's the supply depot for the 4500 Coasties living in the 200 km north of here to the top of the thumb-shaped East Coast at Wharekahika or Hicks Bay.

As far as Coasties are concerned, Gisborne is a separate place. It's where they go more by necessity than preference, to deal with banks, lawyers, courts, supermarkets, farm suppliers, appliance shops—everything they can't get at their local general store.

Though officially excluded, Gisborne is also the start of the East Coast proper: heartland of the Ngati Porou, 40,000-strong and the second largest Maori tribe. Most live away from the region, though about 10,000 are in Gisborne, leaving a few thousand scattered around the Coast's 60-odd marae to guard Ngati Porou turangawaewae.

A few minutes and the town is far behind, replaced by the green and burnt-brown hill country that characterises the Coast. The hills are blotchy from slumping where the land was cleared for farming by colonists in the 1880s. The scars of slips from Cyclone Bola, which in March 1988 sluiced away farmland and rearranged rivers, are all but healed now.

Sponge Bay turn-off holds the first secret to journeying on 35: it is down side roads that the Coast really exists; it is here the traveller will find treasure. The beauty of Sponge Bay bursts upon the eye like privilege. Grey escarpments rise a hundred metres on both sides of the tiny bay, and at their feet frothy seas smother the long reefs that run offshore to Tuamotu Island and its legendary surf spots.

Not many people live on the highway. The very thing that makes the Coast 'The Coast' is the beaches, river mouths and settlements in little bays. A myriad of side-roads run off 35—96 of them heading inland to the forests and sheep and cattle stations of the backblocks, 75 of them toward the sea.

The 15-km stretch from Wainui Beach to Pouawa is my favourite because it hugs the Pacific. In fact, it is the only bit of the road that does so on the eastern half of the Coast. Again today it sighs under the weight of a heavy, sleepy sun. The air is as thick and sweet as honey. The sea is the cobalt blue of deep water, and it glitters in the hard unfiltered light.

From the hills of Makorori and Tatapouri, exactly where horse-drawn coaches laid the first wheel tracks of a coastal route in 1887, you can see Mahia

Forestry is booming and log exports are choking the Port of Gisborne and roads
of the region as this relatively newfound industry takes hold on the East Coast.
Opposite page: A logging ship awaits a berth in Poverty Bay to take on logs
from the stockpiles that are ever present on the city's waterfront.

Peninsula in the south and Gable Islet in the north. Beside the road a few 'freedom campers', with their semi-permanent summer set-ups of tents and tarpaulins, hippie buses and old caravans, are still in occupation. The local authorities grumble about it every year, but free camping is still allowed on much of the Coast—officially only between Labour Weekend in October and Easter in April.

In the hills before Whangara I overtake a schoolbus doing the afternoon drop-off and a family ute jam-packed with groceries and sporting a new TV set in its box.

I'm buffeted by a logging truck and a semi-trailer of squash breaking the speed limit going the other way to Gisborne port. In the flat paddocks of the Whangara Valley I see where the squash is coming from. It's March—harvest time—and there is laughter in the fields. Chain-gangs of young Maori men play passing games with the ripe green footballs as they load them into bins for export to Japan. The 30-odd pickers wear jeans and track pants, bandannas and flax cowboy hats. They have bare muscled chests and tattoos. I'm a stranger, possibly an undercover agent, and they look at each other or the ground when I ask where I can find the boss. Someone on a tractor points me to a farm cottage.

Nohoroa Haapu, 42, is breastfeeding her new baby at the kitchen table, surrounded by books and tax forms and pay envelopes. The last loads of squash and sweetcorn are on their way to market, and she is happy because her organic gardening venture is doing well. The corn will pay $249 a tonne compared with $116 for 1994's non-organic crop. The squash will fetch a similar premium. At last there is vindication for her years of bullying and wheedling the Tapuwai-Whitiwhiti Incorporation to let her phase out chemical fertilisers and pesticides and get organic certification for the 1300-ha tribal farm.

In 1995 Nohoroa cropped 35 ha of flat, chemical-free land, and the following year the whole farm's 5000 sheep and 1200 cattle qualified for the lucrative organic meat market in Europe. Trial plots of trees have been planted for firewood and stock fodder, and hilly sites have been earmarked for berries and vegetables such as potato, kumara and onions.

Her project is a key to the Coast's economic renaissance, she believes. 'It's a humungous goal, I know,' she says, Afro grey hair and magnified eyes behind

Master carver Greg Brightwell works on the tailpiece for a 44-m waka which will require 200 paddlers when it is launched. The project has been delayed by disagreement, but Greg's commitment to it transcends everything else, he says, because it is a work of art that has driven and inspired him for more than five years.

Previous pages: 'Surf City' is one of Gisborne's labels among those who follow the sport of boardriding. In one of three local surfboard factories, New Wave artist Eddie Daly sprays about eighteen new boards a week. The young Ngati Porou surfer has worked in surfboard factories for almost twenty years, and recently launched his own surf clothing label, Nga Ru Toa/ Wave Warrior, as a long-term scheme to escape the health risks of working with foam and fibreglass. Wainui Beach's sand banks produce some of the world's hollowest waves, while Makarori Beach has a long point break that draws surfers the world over.

thick glasses. 'If we can get to a thousand hectares of organic cropping land by the year 2000, that will take care of unemployment. So far we've got probably 150 hectares, including ours and three new blocks undergoing conversion [to organic methods] at Tolaga Bay and Tokomaru Bay. But 1000 hectares is only the beginning. My vision is for the whole Coast.'

The biggest problem with her vision, she says, is men. Men dominate Maori land management. Men have always run the committees that manage the three incorporations of Maori farmland at Whangara, all of it owned by the one Ngatiera hapu or group of interconnected families.

Tapuwai-Whitiwhiti is the smallest block. It has 240 shareholders. Nohoroa inherited her mother's share at the age of five, and, fresh from boarding school at fifteen, 'decided to tootle down to the AGM, and, in my inexperienced youth, stood up and said my piece.' Her presence and words were frowned on, but her grandfather gave silent support by ignoring the challenges of other men. She says she has 'never shut up since', and, after returning to Whangara eleven years ago, was voted onto the Tapuwai-Whitiwhiti and Pakarae committees, and started to implement new ways of working the land.

'Our land has always been our land, even though we've lost touch with what AT taught us,' Nohoroa says. She is referring to Sir Apirana Turupa Ngata, the statesman whose portrait is on our $50 note; the Ngati Porou scholar, writer, orator and politician who created land corporations and revived Maori art and crafts in the first half of this century. 'We've been blessed on the East Coast by never having had our land confiscated or sold out from under us—thanks to our forebears cooperating with the Crown and to AT selling our inland high country to Pakeha leaseholders while retaining the more valuable coastal country.

'We've sustained the land, but we haven't sustained the people. We relied on traditional pastoral farming, but we had no protection—no alternative except forestry, which only sustains Japanese mill owners—when meat and wool prices dropped to uneconomic levels. So the people left the land in a mass exodus to the cities in the fifties and sixties and early seventies. To sustain the people coming back since the eighties is our collective responsibility. I feel it's my responsibility.'

Five minutes away is Whangara Beach, landing place of the first Maori on the Coast. It's a settlement of about twenty houses and shacks and an assortment of wrecks, boats and domestic animals. The central buildings are the lofty marae and meeting house of Paikea the whale-rider, commander of the ocean-going waka *Takitimu* which voyaged here from Hawaiki via Rarotonga. The myths do not agree on whether Paikea's canoe was whale-shaped or an actual whale. The carving on the roof of the meeting house shows the more dramatic rendition: Paikea riding his whale.

Gisborne's 'Golden Mile' is to be found on the shores of Wainui Beach, a few kilometres east of the city. Once a sleepy settlement, the beach is now a sought-after residential area for Gisbornites.

Under a makeshift iron shed on the marae lies another whale—44 m in length, 23 tonnes in weight, lifeless and stranded by disagreement. This giant waka, the largest in the land, was carved from 32 laminated totara logs over the last 5 years. Before going to sea it will need a crew of 200 paddlers or a massive rig of sails. But lack of funds and quarrelling have brought it to a stop for almost twelve months.

Will it make the water? In a way, it doesn't matter. Time waits for everyone, and everything, on the East Coast. I asked for a local opinion and was told that only Tangaroa, god of the sea, knows: 'If it gets on the water and sinks, well, it was supposed to sink, and if it gets on the water and floats, it will float.'

Such fatalism would be laughed at in Auckland. Here it seems as natural as the sun.

Whangara Island is steeped in myth and legend. It was the destination and landing place of Paikea's waka, which brought Polynesian settlers to Aotearoa from Hawaiki hundreds of years ago. Paikea is said to have ridden a whale into Whangara, and made the island its final resting place.
Opposite page: Timeless Whangara village and marae, between Gisborne and Tolaga Bay.

Christenings are occasions for ceremony and celebration, to which friends and family know there is always an open invitation on the East Coast. Nohoroa Haapu and baby Kairoeroe (above) shared their Whangara church christening with Louia Blakeney and baby Honey Lee, with the Reverend Honey Pahau officiating.

2

TOLAGA BAY IS BUSY TODAY. Kids loiter about the main street's strip of a dozen shops, sharing takeaways and jokes; youths outside the pub share a smoke. I'm here to see a woman about aloe vera and a man about a mule.

Tolaga is one of the biggest towns on the Coast: 686 people, a motel, two fast-food joints, a garage, three grocery stores and dairies, a liquor store, a video shop, the pub and the Coast's sole bank. Two cars pause on the bridge into town so their drivers can talk. Ninety years ago, when this bridge was opened, local folk celebrated with a public holiday. So momentous was the occasion that they called out the local brass band, formed a procession of 250 people and treated themselves to a formal lunch and an evening dance.

The Coast's mountainous spine creates a river system that has riddled Highway 35 with bridges—73 in total, 12 of them still single-laned, all of huge local importance.

Living right on 35 by the Tolaga bridge, Ngaio Morrow is 64, a part-time practitioner of aromatherapy and acupressure at the liberal local doctor's medical centre, and an aloe vera grower. She and husband Milton left the Coast in 1950 but came home six years ago to grow aloe vera commercially as a 'retirement lark'. From 100 plants of the Australian *barbadensis* variety they now have 6000 under shade cloth in their quarter-acre plantation. Working to government-approved recipes in their factory cum garage, they manufacture a 'system-cleansing' aloe vera tonic, a gel for human and animal cuts and sores, and

Waipare Homestead, a gracious old kauri homestead built from materials shipped from Auckland to the Coast and brought into Anaura Bay on longboats, is now an open family home doubling as a retreat for people suffering burnout in business.

Organic gardener Gabriel Dominey and her husband Bruce supply the
Tolaga Bay district with free range eggs and chemical-free vegetables, and are
well regarded for their generosity and hard work in the community. They feed
organic vegies to two house cows named June and Pixie, and in turn their milk
is allowed to curd for chicken feed.

moisturising cream and soap. Keeping up with orders from health shops, naturopaths and private customers is difficult; expansion unavoidable.

'We could go into this in a big way if we could find the land,' says Ngaio. My eyes drift to the paddock next door. It's obviously not being farmed. Ngaio reads the question in my mind. 'It makes me mad that the weeds are six feet high and the owners can't agree on a use for it. We wouldn't be opposed to a co-op venture. I feel like kicking their backsides. It's all here. The soil is here. The land is here. But it's all just too iffy for me.'

The age-old Pakeha bugbear: Maori land lying idle. It's an argument I don't feel like getting into right now, so I drive north to find Des McGrannachan for a laugh.

Des and his wife Kathy, the local Plunket nurse, live on a chaotic hectare of machines and animals sandwiched between the highway and the Uawa River. Des was a possum trapper and goat culler, but now, at 46, share-crops maize and corn and uses his tractors to do contract work for farmers. For recreation, he surfcasts on every full moon and hunts runaway red deer—240 of which escaped and went feral in Cyclone Bola, and now provide sport and food in the hills behind Tolaga Bay.

Overlooking the fertile river flats of Tolaga Bay.

'Har, har, har, har,' Des guffaws with squinting, friendly eyes when I say I've come to talk about his mule. Des is wiry, weatherbeaten, bushy-bearded and wears a beanie to cover a thoroughly bald scalp. Hair from the sides of his head is tied back into a ponytail.

'Muley? Why? What do you want to know about him for?'

'Because I heard . . . ' I choose my words carefully, 'that he was . . . an accident.'

'In an accident? Not that I know of.'

'No, I mean he was an accident. Like you weren't expecting him. He was a surprise.'

Des belly-laughs again. Smiles. Sighs. 'All right, come and meet Muley.'

I follow Des to meet the animal rumoured to have been his shameful un-doing at many a social function in this horse-loving district. Behind an over-grown orchard, we first meet Muley's mother, Little One, a fine-looking brown thoroughbred mare, and a winner at the nearby Kaiaua Beach Horse Races, held

'Muley is a cheeky thing,' says Des McGrannachan, but not as cheeky as the donkey that jumped the back fence and made Des the laughing stock of Tolaga Bay. Muley's mum fell pregnant to the undesirable sire after winning prizes at the annual Kaiaua Beach horse races.

Previous pages: Tolaga Bay's 660-m wharf was built in the 1920s to allow ship loading and unloading on all tides, but lost its importance when vehicles arrived on the new coast road. Today it is used mainly by commercial fishermen and boaties, but urgently needs repairs to prevent it being condemned.

annually on New Year's Day. Then here comes Muley, bounding towards us, all legs and jet black. It half-skids to a stop, and I see that, indeed, this creature is half-horse, half-donkey, like nothing I've seen.

That's how it should be, Des says. You don't see mules, because no one who likes horses deliberately has or wants a mule. When Little One got pregnant, Des couldn't work it out. He'd loaned her to someone to ride in the races, and suspected a stallion did the deed there. But she wasn't on heat then, so he was puzzled. It was Des' dad, an old Gisborne farmer, who deduced the sire could only have been Des' donkey in the back paddock. It was further concluded that, because 'Donk' was so short and Little One so tall, he'd straddled a broken fence on a slope to gain his cunning advantage.

'"That bloody donkey," I said,' says Des. '"If it's him he can go!"'

Donk did end up going. Before Muley was born, and the hypothesis finally proven, Donk was trucked to Hawke's Bay to a cattle farm, where he could perform his true role of kicking and biting bulls to keep them under control. But before he got there, Donk was forgotten about and left in the truck, where he died of dehydration. The truck firm, Des says, even had the cheek to ask a hundred dollars for freight. '"Get stuffed!" I told them.'

In a part of the country where every man owns not just a dog but also a horse or two, Des McGrannachan has been laughed at by his fellows. 'But, hey,' he says, fondly stroking his gangly beard, 'I can live with that.'

Last stop: Anaura Bay, ten minutes down another side road. When Sydney Parkinson, Captain Cook's natural historian, wrote in 1769 about the East Coast being 'agreeable beyond description' and 'a second kind of Paradise', I suspect he meant Anaura Bay.

MY LASER SPITS GRAVEL grunting up the corrugations of the hill that isolates Anaura from the highway. The climb finishes in a crescendo of beauty: the white arc of the bay sweeps for three alluring kilometres beneath a bowl of green grass and bush slopes. What Parkinson found is still the same: 'Flowering shrubs intermingled with tall and stately palms fill the air with a most grateful fragrant perfume.' Creeks spill down from the drainages, and on the fertile flats of the shore vegetables and fruit flourish as they did when the *Endeavour* called 226 years ago. Cook's scribe was astonished then at the neatness and luxuriance of the native gardens and the abundance of seafood. Food and hospitality were showered on the English sailors, whereas they got nothing down the coast— which is why they called it Poverty Bay.

At Anaura's south end, an old schoolhouse serves as a camping ground, and a handful of beach houses look out towards Motuoroi Island. Before the white man arrived, Anaura had 2000 inhabitants, and the island its own colony of greenstone workers, who built terraces into the rock so that greenstone weapons and ornaments could be polished using the action of wave and tide. Today, as the terraces erode, fewer than twenty families have the bay to themselves.

In Harry's Bar, resplendent in a black double-breasted suit, white shirt and crimson tie, his greying hair swished back, beard neatly trimmed, Don Blakeney looks the archetypal movie star.

Harry's is the old tack room and farm office of Anaura Bay's gorgeous Waipare Homestead, a rambling colonial kauri villa built in the 1880s. The sheep station it once served reverted to Maori ownership when its lease expired, and the homestead was sold. It sits back from the beach at the northern end of the bay among towering Moreton Bay figs, pohutukawa, giant Norfolk pines and an orchard.

Blakeney, 52, lean, handsome, known to his friends as Scrubbs, presides as lord of the manor. Holding forth in Harry's Bar, an outhouse with oiled kauri walls, a glass of his own rose petal wine in one hand, a Rothmans in the other, Scrubbs is passionate. Tonight's discussion rambles over a range of subjects: his work as a community employment adviser, the book he's reading—*Primitive Christianity*—Waipare's gardens, the surf he rode this morning out beyond his front gate.

Tonight's dinner wine, he announces, is his wife Louia's special blend made from rose petals, rosemary and red clover picked from the roadside. The fresh pesto Scrubbs has made for dinner, from his small commercial plot of basil, is served formally in the front drawing room of the homestead overlooking the grass tennis court, to the sound of breaking surf and a crackling open fire. The pesto comes with steamed karengo, a lettuce-like seaweed, fresh kina (sea eggs) and crayfish—all of it harvested from the bay. For an aperitif, and subsequent nightcaps, Scrubbs pours shotglasses of 37.1-percent proof square gin, an East Coast drink if ever there was one. Sales of it are greater here than anywhere else in the country.

For both its natural and human attractions, Waipare has a constant flow of guests: relations on two sides, old friends from the movie industry, local Maori consulting him for his accounting and business knowledge, teenage dropouts whose parents send them here for direction and motivation, sick people needing

'The country is agreeable beyond description and with proper cultivation might be rendered a second kind of Paradise,' wrote Sydney Parkinson, the natural historian aboard Captain Cook's Endeavour. *Anaura Bay, just north of Tolaga Bay, was one of the places he liked most.*

Sylvia Ashton-Warner described young East Coast school children in her book Teacher as being 'full of take, break, fight and be first,' which could easily refer to these children at the Maungatuna Kura Kaupapa, a 'full immersion' Maori language school near Tolaga Bay.

In the late 1980s, Don Blakeney, ex-movie producer and merchant banker, left
Wellington for a saner life at Anaura Bay with his wife Louia and baby
Honey Lee.

rest, and foreign WOOFers (Willing Workers On Organic Farms) coming to stay free in exchange for work on the 1-ha property.

It's usual for the Blakeney household to be catering for a few extras most nights and maybe a dozen people at weekends. In summer Scrubbs and Louia run garden parties for holidaymakers and visitors, drawn not just by a curiosity to nose around the homestead but also by sales of fresh pesto, a pig on a spit, and showings of pop art and sculpture in the converted stables and coach-house at the bottom of the garden.

So how did Don Blakeney the Dunedin schoolboy dux, the Ernst and Young accountant who became financial controller of P&O in London by the age of 29, the chief executive of the New Zealand Film Commission in its formative years of 1977 to 1981—responsible for the making of *Goodbye Pork Pie* and *Smash Palace*—the producer of the feature film *Utu*, his Arc De Triomphe in the movie business, fetch up on the shores of an isolated bay, surfing, entertaining and making gorse-blossom wine?

Burn-out, he says, musing on the event that both nearly slew him and saved him. Fleeing Wellington in the late 1980s, he travelled to the East Coast beaches he had frequented as a surfer during his youth, chanced upon an ad for Waipare in the real estate columns of the *Gisborne Herald*, and pounced on it with all the money he could scratch together.

Scrubbs the Coastie has drunk deeply of the local culture and become a man with a mission, for the last few years spending most of his time on contract to the Labour Department's Community Employment Group. Like an itinerant minister, he travels Highway 35 every day, dispensing business advice, helping organise finance, writing business plans and doing accounts for mainly Maori individuals and community groups.

The Coasties he has helped get into business include forestry contractors, grocery store owners, music teachers, tourism operators, surfboard makers and traders in flowers, essential oils, arts and crafts, possum skins and seaweed.

Perhaps the Coast is a place where philosophy and ethics naturally run deep, or perhaps Scrubbs is still on the rebound from the heady days of hustle and spin. He takes the local tikanga—protocols— seriously, reprimanding me when I inadvertently break a custom over the taking of seafood. A couple of years ago he dismantled his computer, because he felt his already TV-free stepson, Dwight, then aged eight, was spending too much time playing computer games instead of reading or conversing, making music or listening to travellers around the kitchen table in the evenings.

Being without a computer is no big deal for his business, he tells me, because he has always done his writing and financial planning, including calculations and spreadsheets, by arithmetic and long-hand. 'It helps me figure my figures and think things out,' he says. Many a client has sat through tedious budgeting exercises in his stately study, which faces the sea, cats curled up at his feet, embers of a fire glowing in the hearth. You soon realise how effective it is to hand-craft budgets and cashflow forecasts the slower Scrubbs way, talking through every detail, sipping brewed coffee.

When a real estate agent approached Scrubbs recently to see if he would sell Waipare, talking of clients who wanted to make it a holiday house and park their yacht in the bay, his message was blunt: 'This isn't a rich man's paradise. It's a community resource. The reality is that it is better for local people, tangata whenua, to be here than it is for anyone else.'

Such values are expressed in all his business plans, and especially his tourism project proposals. He speaks of the need for Maori to approach tourism developments with confidence and cunning, rather than being pushed and manipulated by external market or investment pressures.

Certainly Waipare, for all its visitor attractions, has none of that. Louia, the bubbly, witty domestic head of the household, makes sure of it. As well as applying her gourmet chefing skills, learned in cafés and Gisborne wineries, Louia also directs proceedings in the vegetable gardens, herb garden, flower beds, orchard, home brewery and—out front—Waipare's kai moana fishing grounds. She dispenses natural medicines and herbal remedies for both human and farm animal healing. For the bumptious and deserving, she reserves her 'haunted' room, one of seven second-storey bedrooms, and makes sure the mystique is thick when she ushers them upstairs.

One night over the square gin, Scrubbs explained to me his philosophy for Waipare. 'Our life is so rich that we have to be careful. It's a taonga that isn't given away easily. You can't just come here and get it. You have to respect it, then you will have earned it. The whole of the East Coast is a taonga to be treasured and protected from outside exploitation,' he says. 'The East Coast is not a bungy jump.'

Yes, I muse on my way back to 35, this is a taonga. It feels good that Waipare is no longer the domain of landed gentry. The consummate 1990s mix of things Maori and Pakeha? I don't really know. Paradise? Definitely.

I pass the house of Waipare's nearest neighbours, a 1950s-styled weatherboard box with car wrecks, chooks and a few pigs in the yard. 'We haven't got much,' a woman from the bay told me in Harry's Bar, her words still ringing in my mind. 'We're as poor as can be. But we live the lives of kings.'

Mickey Harrison picks puha beneath the vines at Hikuwai Vineyard—a vital, strong-flavoured ingredient for any meat-and-vegetable 'boil-up' worthy of the name in this part of the world. Mickey was helping with the catering at a tangi on Waipiro Bay Marae.

3

ANOTHER SUNNY DAY, another day on a road chiselled into the East Coast hill country like the lines of a moko. I stop to the sound of hooting, yelling children outside a woody country schoolyard at Mangatuna. It's like stepping back in time 50 years to a scene from Sylvia Ashton-Warner, the pioneer educator, whose books *Teacher* and *I Passed This Way* describe life in the East Coast's 'native schools' (a term she hated).

'Young Maori children,' she writes, 'are the only real clue we have to what a Maori warrior was like in the past, before European discipline is clamped down on them.' All the children I can see are Maori, primary age, and, like Sylvia's young warriors, they are 'full of take, break, fight, and be first'.

About 30 of them are running in a circular relay, cheering their mates on. They pound around a concrete court in front of the two-classroom school building; little girls in hand-me-down dresses, hundred-dollar Doc Martens, bare feet; little boys in baggy shorts, Rasta T-shirts, basketball boots, bare feet.

'Sir, sir, their team's cheating,' one complains, but the teacher isn't listening.

They're supposed to be taking off at intervals to the signal of their teacher, Jack Tuhiwai, 50-ish, white-shirt-and-tie, white boater-style sunhat, dark dress trousers. 'Tahi, *trrrrreee!*, rua, *trrrrreee!*, toru, *trrrrreee!*, wha, *trrrrreee!*' he counts and blasts on a silver whistle. It's bedlam.

This is a thriving Kura Kaupapa Maori, one of the new generation of

With time on their hands and nothing much to do, Tokomaru Bay family Michael and Epe Paiti and baby Elijah rely on Michael's income from seasonal pine tree planting to make ends meet. Employment is scarce on the East Coast, with a majority of adults on the dole or some other form of benefit.

Photographer Jill Carlyle and her partner Al Mount have preserved an old schoolhouse as a home and workplace outside Tokomaru Bay. Jill's love of photography, art and horses blends easily into the lifestyle of the East Coast. Opposite page: Its empty buildings and streets sometimes make Tokomaru Bay seem like a ghost town.

Waima potter Baye Riddell moulds local clays into ethnic designs using the old Tokomaru Bay Freezing Works as his workshop and gallery. Baye has won scholarships to travel and exhibit his pottery in the United States and exchange ideas with native American potters in Arizona.

Opposite page: The happy-go-lucky highway passes just in front of—but right through the heart of—two young Coasties with nothing much to do but suck on a Steinie on a quiet winter's night at Tokomaru Bay.

'total immersion' Maori language schools, designed by Maori for Maori. All instruction is in Maori, and includes teaching of customs and cultural tradition, art and craft, and spiritual values. There are six Kura on the Coast. This one is a great success. In a year the roll has gone from 19 to 39, with most pupils coming daily by car and a parent-funded bus from Tolaga Bay. In the main, they come because of Jack, who in 1994 returned to his birthplace after 25 years of secondary teaching all around New Zealand.

'These kids thrive in the Kura Kaupapa environment because it gives them the confidence to stand up and be counted,' Jack says. 'Throw them in the mainstream education system and they'd be lost because they haven't got the whanau around them.' With an A-grade teacher, a teacher-aid and a resource person to help him, Jack's Kura takes credit for reopening a perfectly suitable government school building and property which were shut down under the State system.

At Mangaroa Station for lunch, up the Waiau Road, Graeme Williams gives me the low-down on the dynasty of his family, who own half a dozen sheep and cattle stations on the Coast. Graeme, 34, is a fifth-generation descendant of Bishop William Williams, the Anglican missionary who brought Christianity to the Coast in 1840.

'Sure we get criticised because people think we inherited all this land, but I disagree with that. People say, "You're all right, you get born into a farm and get given it," but that's a load of crap. Your parents don't just suddenly move off the land into town on fresh air. We've got what we've got because we work hard.'

Graeme says some of his uncles went broke guaranteeing loans for Maori farmers in the twenties and thirties, and hopes people still remember that.

He tells me he was 'as thick as pig-shit' at boarding school at Wanganui Collegiate, so he went mustering and shearing. In a hut on Mesopotamia Station

down south, he read a poem scribbled on the wall and decided to write rhymes of his own. 'Not like Sam Hunt though . . . his stuff does nothing for me . . . poetry has to rhyme and make people laugh.'

Like 'Toast to the Coast', which he recites between mouthfuls of spaghetti and toast as he autographs a copy of his self-published book, *Ribtickling Rhymes*, for me to take away:

> *Now we know it's off the beaten track,*
> > *and to get there is a trek.*
> *And it's not a yuppie's haven,*
> > *with computers or high-tech.*
> *And the pace of things it's casual,*
> > *your life it will not wreck.*
> *As you haven't ten thousand people,*
> > *breathing down your neck!*

Outside Tokomaru Bay, I drop in on Rob McKenzie to find out about his thriving waka ama (outrigger canoe) club at Tokomaru Bay. The nationwide revival of waka sport among Maori has come to the Coast in recent years thanks to this man—a strapping six-foot-something Pakeha shearer and beekeeper who shifted here from the South Island sixteen years ago. He jokes that he expects to qualify as a local 'any day now'.

With one 6-seat racing canoe—a 14-m fibreglass version of the traditional carved wooden craft—Rob trains 38 teenagers every week on the sea. They travel away to compete, charged by the excitement and pride of paddling alongside scores of boats. 'It's a bit more than the sum of its parts when these kids are on the water,' he says. 'They get the connection between effort and reward, and get fired up. I get a buzz out of it, too.'

Outside Rob's home, a run-down 70-year-old farmhouse, his good shearing mate Boy Raihania is passing up new spouting to a plumber. As I go, he tells me to make no mistake: Rob McKenzie *is* a local. 'Everyone likes him,' Boy says. 'He's easy-going, he's massive with kids. You've got to fit with the life up here, eh, not fit the life to you. Rob does that, eh. Tooo much!'

'Tooo much!' I can hear myself thinking when I slip away. 'Too much!' or 'Tu meke!' is a favoured saying on the Coast.

I STOP FOR A BREW of thick coffee at Tokomaru Bay with Jill Carlyle. In the Waiapu Community Arts Council art and craft shop, one of six main-street businesses, a young Japanese couple staying at The House of the Rising Sun, the local backpackers', ask Jill if she's got any greenstone tikis. No, she hasn't, but she's got some very nice carved bone ones made in Ruatoria and priced from

As the sun rises across Waipiro Bay, Corporal Leo Harrison awaits the dawn parade on Anzac Day at Iritekura War Memorial meeting house. Home from Waiouru Army Camp for the parade, Corporal Harrison was present for the unveiling of his father's headstone and to receive his J Force Medal, awarded posthumously, 50 years after Japan's occupation by New Zealand soldiers.

Previous pages: Between sun-soaked hills and wooded valleys, Highway 35 always returns to the sea—with places like Tokomaru Bay luring travellers to stop and stay awhile.

only $50. They decline. 'I suppose if I'd had a plastic tiki they'd have bought it,' Jill mutters. Business is slow today: she's sold a couple of postcards and a flax kit.

Jill, 38, was born at Waipiro Bay and raised at Ruatoria, where her parents had a drapery business for 40 years. Her passions are horseriding and black-and-white photography. To date, she's shot 550 rolls of film, mostly of local Maori, whom she counts as family. 'These people have a beautiful simplicity about them, no pretentiousness at all,' she says. Jill was halfway through a book on the Coast with the writer Barry Mitcalfe when he died in 1984; some day she'll finish it, she says, or she'll donate her unfinished work to the Gisborne Museum.

She and partner Al Mount, a writer, live in an old one-room schoolhouse, a few kilometres west of town, which they get to by fording a creek on foot. They park their HQ Holden beside Highway 35 and never lock it. Says Al: 'If Marx and Engels and Trotsky had come to the East Coast, they'd have said, "Forget the revolution, let's stay here—socialism is already working fine here!"'

A stone's throw away, I make an astonishing find. Squatting clandestinely behind a screen of trees less than a hundred metres from the road are the bones of a sailing ship—in fact, a replica of the 23-m coastal schooner *Miro*, which traded on the East Coast and Auckland coastline at the turn of the century.

The owner-builder doesn't want to be identified, paranoid he could get into trouble with Income Support. I wonder if, instead of being harassed for his transgressions, he deserves a hand-out to finish such a worthwhile project. On an unbelievably small budget over four years he has cut and milled all his timber, salvaged and rebuilt an engine, and created the 40-tonne wooden hull—mostly alone and barefooted, with hand tools and steam boxes.

He is an ancient mariner possessed by a dream. Or a demon. The project has consumed a marriage and more borrowed money than he can afford, but he still yearns to sail the Coast like the salts of old. There's at least a year of work to go before stepping the 20-m masts. All going well, the second *Miro* will freight produce and tourists to make a living off the Coast.

I'm booked on the maiden voyage; I'm a dreamer too.

Te Puia Springs, with views of Mt Hikurangi to the west and Waipiro Bay to the east, is a sanctuary of stately trees, a lake, mineral springs and 189 people. The town smells sulphuric, and for a dollar I soak in a mineral bath in the gardens of the pub to see if it's true that these waters are 'most exhilarating and possess curative properties of a high order' as written in a 1924 travel guide.

Certainly, after a couple of cold beers in a hot pool I feel a little exhilarated, but for curative powers I think I'd be better off at Te Puia's hospital, a 40-bed complex on the edge of the lake. The hospital serves the whole Coast, and is talking of making a bid for independence from the Gisborne-based Tairawhiti Area Health Board, if it can get government approval. Good luck.

*Recalling wars past and friends and family who marched off to fight them,
elders assemble on the Waipiro Bay marae for Anzac Day commemorations.*

Her face lit by reflected sunlight, Connie Henare concentrates on the task of
sorting freshly shorn wool at Opiki Station.
Opposite: On many East Coast sheep stations, docking is still done by the
cruder but quicker cut-and-bite method—as practised by Base Westrupp on
Kiteroa Station—which is believed to carry less risk of infection than the use
of rubber rings. It also produces 'mountain oysters'—a local delicacy fetching
$50 for an ice-cream container full. The lambs' tails are eaten too: throw them
in a fire until well done, scrape the burnt skin off and invite all your friends
around for a feed!

4

THE ROAD DRAWS ME ON. I skip the detour to Waipiro Bay—once a coach trail staging post and a thriving port. Now it's a ghost town with a population of 99 and a point break that attracts surfers the world over.

Nearby Ruatoria looks worn out, too. Its better days were the 1930s, when they called it the capital of the Coast and several thousand people lived here. Today it's a quarter that size, and has the media reputation of a Beirut or a Belfast. During the last 10 years the town has been physically and emotionally blighted by a cultish Rastafarian uprising: nearly 30 counts of arson, family infighting and bloodshed. Peace reigns at present, and people prefer not to talk about the matter.

One related topic that occupies many a conversation here is the local cannabis industry. Graham and Robyn Neilsen, owners of the Ruatoria garage, claim the cops killed the town's cashflow when they pulled all the weed in their annual summer recovery exercise. 'I don't know why they bother,' Graham says.

He and Robyn, who live east of the town at Tikapa, where electricity still hasn't arrived for the twenty-odd households, have invented a solar power system to run an entire household and say it's an alternative source of income for them. For about $10,000 they can install solar power in a house and stop power bills forever. 'Everyone wants the natural alternative, but finance is the problem. The banks don't like lending to the unemployed.'

The answer to unemployment, according to Ngati Porou tribal bosses at the runanga headquarters in Ruatoria, is forestry. They have their hearts set on it

Myth and legend come to life at Ngata Memorial College, Ruatoria, during a stage production of Witi Ihimaera's play The Whale Rider.

as the hope of the future. Manager Ned Ihaka says there are 102,000 ha of Maori-owned land in the tribe—50,000 to 60,000 ha of which would be better off planted in pine trees than left as manuka and kanuka scrub or farmland. He says work schemes, horticulture experiments and alternative land use are Band Aids that come from an ambulance mentality. 'Our land owners have to get real,' he says. 'The only real means of employment and wealth creation here is forestry.'

That wealth is still just a promise—and decades away—for most of the tribe. Recently the runanga signed a $60 million deal with a Korean forestry company which does not abide by the Forest Accord, an environmental agreement that provides for preservation of all native and regenerating native bush. The Koreans will plant 10,000 ha of Ngati Porou land in pines over the next five years, claiming their own environmental charter and a two-for-one policy means for every tree felled another two are planted. There will be immediate employment for labourers to plant the new radiata, future job creation in pruning and thinning and, when the trees are mature, the possibility of a processing facility being built.

In the meantime, Social Welfare pays the bills. From Gisborne to Hicks Bay there are nearly 1000 adults on the dole—probably more than half the adult population. Dole day, Thursday, is a boom day in Gisborne's supermarkets, toy shops and fast-food outlets. In townships like Ruatoria it's also the day for 'Battens Up'—a lottery where you buy a numbered batten and wait hours for a series of draws for meat, produce, clothing and appliances. It's the social highlight of the week.

Don Blakeney says that lack of money is one of the reasons the Coast is so lovely—it makes everyone equal. 'I don't begrudge anyone $130 a week. Hell, what's the dole? It's not depriving the taxpayer of $130. One crooked tax deal by the white collar boys can diddle the taxpayer of $130 million!'

A GHOST WOKE us just before dawn, scattering Rastafarians in all directions. It brought a sudden end to the three-day religious gathering to which I'd been invited at Whareponga marae, south of Ruatoria.

The marae sits beside a lonely pebble beach littered with driftwood at the mouth of a quiet green valley. I was a guest of the notorious East Coast Rastafarian sect known for its dreadlocks and full-face moko and fearsome

Like father, like son, like grandson—Eru Paenga raises his mokopuna Henare traditionally on the marae at Waiomatatini while Henare's parents serve in the navy, based at Devonport, Auckland.

His eyes alive with pride as he talks of his soon-to-be-born child,
Rastafarian Whare Taukamo works in a Ruatoria workshop
where he is handcrafting a wooden crib.

'My moko is my number plate by which Jah will know me when he returns for his chosen few,' says Stryker Kupenga, elder of the Rastafarian sect at Ruatoria. During a three-day retreat, followers imbibed the sacred herb and endured the tattooist's needle as part of Rasta ritual. Clockwise from top left: a cannabis plant plucked for the festivities; King Glory steels himself while tattooist Hone Heeney does the job; Hannah rocks her baby to sleep in the meeting house at Whareponga; Stryker Kupenga ministers the Word.

crimes. I was there in peace to celebrate the birthday of His Imperial Majesty Emperor Haile Selassie, Ethiopia's deceased ruler and divine head of Rastafarianism. It was a weekend of cooking, eating, tattooing, reasoning, singing and resting by fire and candlelight in the meeting house and kitchen of the old Maori pa.

'Now is a time when there is a thin line of peace for the Rastaman, but the good fight is still going on,' they tell me. They see themselves as knights between crusades, and, for the time being, this marae is their round table.

Etched all over their bodies are swords, shields, scrolls, scriptures and flames. Theirs is a holy war, they say, and they chant and sing to contain the pain of the tattoo needle and the pain of their hearts.

The ghost's arrival in the wee hours of the third morning was reported by Stryker Kupenga, the Rasta kaumatua who presided over formal whaikorero (speechmaking) during the weekend. Stryker was asleep on the concrete floor in front of the kitchen fireplace when the ghost came and told him of a death in the valley. In a separate visitation, there was a ruckus when a stranger burst upon Stryker and demanded the Rastafarians leave, because a funeral party was arriving at daybreak, and they didn't want the Rastas hanging round.

Stryker Bonecrusher Lavender Marijuana Kupenga Jones—the Rastas' name for the 55-year-old seer of their hybrid sect—is also a Ringatu minister who is said to have spent three years as a recluse in the bush alone with God and his Bible. 'Afterwards, when I joined the Rastamen, my family said I was mad,' says Stryker, his face tattooed according to local Rasta custom. 'But I listen not to man but to the word of God which says in Revelation chapter 22, "They will see his face, and his name will be on their foreheads."'

At first light, Stryker brought instant action to our camp with one word: 'Mahi!' We were to clean up and go. In 30 minutes, mattresses were stacked, belongings gathered, floors swept, dishes done. For those quick enough there was a standing breakfast of leftovers from the weekend 'boil-up'—wild beef, spuds and puha. The 25-odd Rastas fled on horses and in old cars back up the gravel road through the valley to 35.

I stopped in the bush to help three of the dreads, as they call themselves, chainsaw and load replacement firewood for the marae. Looking at the mokoed, laughing faces of Hone, Whare and Chiefy as we felled, hauled and cut up manuka logs, it was hard to see them as arsonists, drug lords, social vermin. Such are their labels.

'You coming back to see us for ta moko, Hone?' Chiefy jested, asking me for the third or fourth time that weekend if I wanted a tattoo. 'No, bro, next time,' I lied.

'You make sure you write good about us then, eh Hone,' Chiefy said, less frivolously this time. I knew what he meant.

They need good PR. They had told me so during a business discussion. They've formed the Kirikiritatangi Charitable Trust with help from Employment Service and Labour Department people. Their aims are to run commercial vegetable gardens and to build their own marae with low-cost adobe housing. They hope to get funding support now that they have a legal structure and plans on paper for self-sufficiency. Getting people to believe them, they say, is the biggest battle.

The Rastas of Ruatoria first made headlines in the mid-1980s when family feuding, beatings, retaliations and extremism led to 27 cases of arson running to millions of dollars—churches, school buildings, businesses, houses, the courthouse, the police station. The controversy was fuelled by the kidnapping of a constable, a macabre Rasta beheading, vigilante patrols and the fatal shooting of Rasta leader Kara (Chris) Campbell by a local farmer, who was acquitted. Prison sentences were slapped on many of the Rastas, but a core has kept the sect alive.

When I reached the Whareponga roadhead around ten in the morning, I was sweaty and stunk of manuka and marijuana smoke. I hadn't changed or washed in four days.

Still mentally stricken by the ghost incident, I was stripped to my undies, lathered in soap, brushing my teeth and cleaning my breath with Pepsodent, thigh deep in the Waikohu Stream beneath a bridge on Highway 35, when I heard a car coming. This trip I had no vehicle of my own, and needed to hitch home to Gisborne.

What I heard was instantly recognisable. This cannon-shot backfiring, metallic shuddering joke of a car, a broken-down 30-year-old Morris 1100, had attacked me already on this trip. Three days before, I'd ridden 20 km by horseback to the Rasta hui in the company of Stryker and Rasta leader Hone Heeney. For four hours we trotted along quiet roads in the overshadowing presence of snowcapped Mt Hikurangi, talking off and on about lives, families and beliefs.

'We are the rainbow people of the last days,' Stryker said, 'direct-line descendants from the seed of Elijah right through to the Lion of Judah—Haile Selassie-I—228th direct descendant from Jesse, father of King David. Jesse was the blackest man the world had ever seen. We are the remnant of the lost tribe of Israel, and this land is the holy land, and Hikurangi is the sacred mountain . . .'

Hone interrupted: 'And from that mountain a white horse will appear carrying the man who is coming when his time is right to give us victory over our enemy.'

Stryker chanted karakia and sang waiata as we rode. No bellicose details followed, only the rhythmic jolting of my mount, a stallion called Catch A Fire, which made me torpid and sleepy. We were well down the Whareponga valley

Bible study during the Rasta retreat or 'ra'.

when the rusty red Morris snapped me out of it. For a split-second I thought Armageddon had begun. Out of nowhere it came blasting and clattering around a blind corner, spooked Catch A Fire and had me hyperventilating in an instant.

Here it was again, with its herniating death rattle.

By the time I dressed and climbed up to 35 from my bathing hole, the 1100 had stopped and gone silent right on the bridge. Its hapless driver was all smiles and big white teeth when I appeared. 'Ki'ora, bro,' he grinned, 'you wanna lift?' I was incredulous, but accepted. 'Chuck your gear in the back, bro. Jump in, bro. Would you like a cuppa tea, bro?'

That sounded good. 'Thanks.'

'We'll just have to wait for my cousin Thomas, though. He's coming in his car.'

On the Coast you learn to go with the flow, not to ask questions sometimes, and to wait. A black car, old as the Morris, appeared on the bridge with

cousin Thomas in it. He pulled up and got out with a length of number eight fencing wire, freshly cut. He and Harry tied it to the cars as a tow-rope, and we took off in our respective vehicles, Harry and I merrily making our acquaintance as we jerked along behind Thomas.

Five km down the road we stopped at Hiruharama (Jerusalem) marae and the housing area, Te Papakainga O Waitakaro. Harry and his young wife and kids live in a garage at the back of Harry's brother's house.

Over cups of tea, poured white and sugary from the pot, Harry opened up. 'Seen you on the horse the other day, eh. You been down at Whareponga with the dreads?' Yes, I said. 'I was s'posed to be there, eh, getting masked up for ta moko.' Harry joined the Rastas ten years ago, then a teenager and the youngest of the original dreads. He'd been planning to get a full face moko for years, and this year's ra—the annual gathering—was meant to be his time. But when he heard a journalist and photographer were attending, he scarpered. Too shy, he said, and so were a dozen other dreads who didn't attend on our account. I felt bad. I had intruded and spoiled their weekend. I tried to apologise.

Harry became lucid. 'I was there when the trouble went down. I remember the day a Jamaican Rastaman came and told us we had to forsake our cultural

On the southern banks of the Waiapu River, Tui Banks stands beside a memorial to his father Alf, who drowned after riding into the river on horseback to slash his mark on a totara log which had been washed downstream by a flood.
Opposite page: Driftwood at Rangitukia, an isolated idyll near East Cape.

Life occurs on the byways and sideroads of Highway 35, where lack of traffic makes youngsters free to roam on their way home from a Saturday rugby match at Rangitukia.
Opposite page: St Mary's Church at Tikitiki is one of the finest Maori churches in New Zealand. It was built in 1924 and consecrated in 1926 as a memorial to Ngati Porou soldiers who died in the First World War. Today it is a home for various denominations, including Anglicans and Ringatu.

Previous pages: Indigo hues crown sacred Mt Hikurangi in the heartland of Ngati Porou country near Ruatoria.

ways if we wanted to be real Rastas. We didn't like what he said, so he jumped on the wind and was gone again. All he really wanted was some weed.' Harry recalled the beatings, and the beheading of a young member of the group who'd been 'playing games' with the leadership. He believed these incidents were justified as internal law and order. 'An eye for an eye, bro, that's how it's always been. No one questions it.'

After Harry's, I got a ride with a clean-cut young Mormon named Eddie Tuhoro. He told me Mormon and Ringatu followers shared the belief that the Maori people were descendants of the lost tribe of Israel. If the Rastas were following Ringatu teaching, he surmised, it was because they identified with the founder of the religion, Te Kooti Rikirangi Te Turuki, the warrior rebel who massacred 60 people at Matawhero, near Gisborne, after escaping from exile on the Chatham Islands in 1868.

Eddie was right. 'Ringatu is the closest English interpretation we can get to Ras Tafari,' leader Heeney told me at Whareponga. 'We were cast out of our families and homes and hunted like the Ku Klux Klan, as they did to Te Kooti and to Ihu Karaiti [Jesus Christ]. Only the vigilantes didn't have white hoods, they had motorbike helmets and baseball bats, and came to our houses and called out, "C'mon, boy, we're gonna get you."

'The fires were retaliations. We knew we would be persecuted, and so for seven years we went through prisons, and now we've learned how to live amongst people. We just want to live as trouble-free as possible until the end when Armageddon comes, when the white horse and its rider, who is living among us now just waiting for his time, will give the call to rise up for Jah. Jah is coming from the holy mountain Hikurangi, and the righteous will enter this holy land from the south gate at Pouawa and the west gate at Opotiki.'

Highway 35: the highway to heaven.

5

STEAMY MIST AND RAIN swirled in the treetops, and a torrent of chocolate-coloured floodwater greeted me in a clearing where the muddy bridle track I had hiked from Rangitukia crossed the Waiora Stream, deep in the bush near East Cape and East Island. I had come to meet a mystic and hermit named Nig Manuel, who spends half of each year camped here with his horses and dogs, living off the land.

I started across the chundering creek, chest deep with my pack held above my head. My splashing set the dogs barking, and an eerie hooded figure appeared on a knoll in the middle of the camp. He was wrapped in a cloak of canvas, and threw it off when he saw me coming. I could see why they call him Nig: blacker complexion than most, matted black dreadlocks, droopy black moustache, tatty black skier's overalls and sleeveless black jersey.

His barrel chest and muscular arms were like Popeye's, and his teeth and big round eyes flashed white as he locked a fierce stare on me. Half crouching with one foot forward in a haka stance, he let out a cry that echoed around the valley. 'Tee-heyyyyyy mauri oraaaah! Tee-heyyyyyyy mauri oraaaah!' He grabbed me by my wet arms, then reached up and clasped the back of my head, pulling my nose against his for a prolonged, wet hongi. 'Ka pai, Hone,' he said. 'I didn't think you would come in this weather. Tooo much, bro, tooo much.'

For eighteen hours we lay on wire-wove beds without mattresses and crouched by an open fire under his A-framed tarpaulin bivvy, talking with understanding as the rain pelted down. The dogs huddled under our beds, and two horses stood still outside next to an old plough and an earthen rua where Nig

A lone rider has the beach to himself at East Cape, mainland New Zealand's eastern extremity.

'I talk to the rains and listen to the heavens,' says Nig Manuel, who lives off the land near East Cape, with Champ, his white stallion, to pull his plough and take him to church on Sundays. Nig is planning a tourism venture in which people would be able to experience his back-to-nature lifestyle. 'In my heart I want to turn this into a place for people to study Maori medicine, a rehab centre for drug and alcohol victims, a place to come for peace and quiet.' Opposite page: Inside Nig Manuel's tarpaulin bivvy during rains at the Makaikatoa bush camp near East Cape.

stores his potato, kumara, kamo kamo, fern roots and corn. In sacks in the creek he keeps fermenting corn for porridge. We sipped black tea and nibbled on burnt, baked roke roke (purple potato) and licorice all-sorts. 'In the hills of holy privacy,' Jack Kerouac wrote in a story about the vanishing hobo, 'there's nothing nobler than to put up with a few inconveniences for the sake of absolute freedom.'

Absolute freedom is what Nig's lifestyle is all about. At 42, he has been back on his family's 250-ha property called Makaikatoa (plenty of food) for 5 years. Prior to that he tried living in Wellington for a few years doing concrete work on high-rise buildings. But booze, drugs and a lag in Wi Tako prison made him wake up and brought him to Christ. His aging mother brought him home to Makaikatoa, and showed him where she had cast his pito—his umbilical cord—telling him to centre his life on the Waiora's living waters.

Now Nig wants to bring others here, to share with them his love of te reo Maori ('Now that I'm home I'm losing my English tongue!'), his Ringatu religion and his interest in natural Maori medicine. A planned tourist venture will involve horseriding, camping in the bush and on Te Pito Beach near East Cape lighthouse, gathering and eating the wild food of the land, sharing the stories of Paikea and exploring sacred sites like a perfectly round tarn on Kautuku Hill where Paikea established a whare wananga—a place of higher learning.

'I'm here as the kaitiaki, the guardian of the land,' Nig says, as we rest our horses atop a craggy lookout above Kautuku Tarn, ringed like an eye by blackened raupo. 'We're sitting on a million-dollar deal if you see it through Pakeha eyes. But that's not what this is about. This land must stay as it is.'

From Nig's, the bucolic road rolls on. That sense of life arrested in mid-breath is ever-present in the outer reaches of the Coast. At Te Araroa, its skyscraper bluff overhanging alluvial flats with the sea in an uproar beyond, I search out Arewhana Street, named after a circus elephant which died and was buried here in the 1930s. But there's no sign of anything except the street name.

The East Coast's general stores serve as community centres as well as shopping centres.
Opposite page: Hine Karaka, Ngati Porou.

Dedicating a new baby to the Lord, Pastor Arthur Baker (hands behind back) leads an Apostolic Church service at Hinerupe meeting house. The preacher, who rides a Harley-Davidson, has overcome arson and persecution to keep his church alive, and keeps exhorting his flock to open their homes and their lives for the sake of evangelism on the East Coast.

Lottin Point, where the Raukumara Range dives into the Pacific Ocean, and the rocky shoreline and deep water support an outstanding fishery that attracts sports fishermen from around the world.

I stop at the old Ministry of Works depot, where essential oil is extracted from manuka scrub by a tribal trust trading as Manex Natural Solutions. They make a range of skin oils, creams, lip balm and soap, and have plans for a new factory employing a dozen people. Company chairman Syd Clarke, the local councillor, tells me they recently had a visit from Anita Roddick, The Body Shop magnate. She was looking at making an investment in Manex, but felt the company and place 'weren't Third World enough' to fit with her corporate ideology. Everyone laughed when they heard that, Syd says.

It's a drowsy Sunday morning when I step into church for the Apostolic service on the Hicks Bay Marae. I'd heard many times that this Pentecostal Christian movement—headed by a hard-case preacher who rides a Harley-Davidson—had converted a number of Rastafarians to their faith. One ex-Rasta convert is married to the pastor's daughter; I'd met him sitting on a sofa at the movies in the tiny multiplex cinema of Te Araroa Holiday Park.

Dressed today in a suit and tie, Pastor Arthur Baker, whose flock of about 200 meets at a succession of services on a half-dozen marae along the Coast, stamps his bikie boots and yells in a hell-fire and damnation sermon to the wide-eyed congregation of about 30. 'We would all like better houses and better cars and better jobs,' he preaches, 'but Jesus said do not lay up treasures for yourselves in this life. Jesus said seek ye first my kingdom. Change your focus, brothers and sisters, and look up. Yes, we're in a wilderness here and, yes, it is hard sometimes. But God knows we're here. We're here to tell others. Open up your lives and your homes and share what you have with the lost and the needy all around us.'

The believers clap and shout their agreement: 'Amen!' 'Praise the Lord!' 'Right on, brother!' These Coasties are a selfless lot, I thought.

A few months later, I had the same thought when I learned that preacher Baker and his family had lost their Potaka home and possessions in an act of arson or retribution for a stand by members of the church on a moral issue.

A young married man in the church had discovered that his wife was having a secret affair with a team-mate from the Hicks Bay Rugby Club. On principle, the aggrieved husband refused to play alongside the man who had wronged him.

Then his four natural brothers, who were also in the team, supported him by standing down from the team as well. For a team that struggles to field a full side every year, this represented an attack on the ranks. 'I was called to a meeting of local community elders, who blamed the church for the problem,' Pastor Baker told me. 'I told them it was a personal choice by the individuals concerned, and not a matter for church intervention. Three days later, while we were attending church, worshipping the Lord, someone torched our home.'

The fire razed the Bakers' secluded farmhouse to the ground. Among the heirlooms lost were the pastor's many books, a lifetime of study and sermon notes, a valuable stamp collection, family photo albums, a Rolex watch and pieces of furniture made in Scotland by Arthur's cabinetmaker grandfather. 'I'll never forget standing in the ashes, saying to myself, "Blow it, let it go, my life doesn't consist in material things." This is just persecution, and it could get worse, but it's to be expected for those who follow the living God.'

For months afterwards the Bakers lived in the undamaged garage beside the ashen remains of their home. They shared the concrete floor space with Arthur's prized Harley-Davidson, a gift he received in answer to prayer some years before. It escaped the fire by being double-locked and secured in the shed. Neither the house nor its contents were insured.

News of the Bakers' 'persecution' reached church people around New Zealand via the national Christian newspaper *Challenge Weekly*. The rally call brought donations totalling $11,000. That money plus proceeds from the sacrificial sale of the motorbike have since enabled the Bakers to buy another home, out of the district at Ruatoria. After the fire, the pastor said, church members were subjected to more persecution within the Hicks Bay community, and younger Apostolics wanted to rise up and fight back. Arthur: 'Our elders told them to cool it, and fortunately everyone did. In my heart now I feel more of a drive and love for those who did this to me and my family. Whoever they are, I've got to win them for the Lord.'

FROM HICKS BAY, Highway 35 turns inland for 30 km, away from the east to a buffer zone of bush and rock forming the vast Wharekahika, Waikura and Potaka forestry and farming district.

Good fortune laid a path of valleys through most of it—a sawtooth

Red Duigan—for more than twenty years a fencer and horseman on the East Coast—dresses a wild pig caught in the hills behind Hicks Bay. Last year Red and his horsetrekking business partner Grim Stanbridge bagged more than 80 boars, many of which were bartered for other necessities of life.

extension of the Raukumaras. No shops. No cellphones. Just schools—one of them exclusively for the twenty-odd kids on sheep and cattle stations in the Waikura Valley.

These are the borderlands, where the tribes of Ngati Porou and the Whanau a Apanui of the Bay of Plenty meet and marry, where progress arrives last on the Coast. Here the tyranny of distance and isolation from the rest of New Zealand, the very thing that has outlawed the Coast for so long, still seems its best friend.

Whakakotahitanga (joining together as one), the association of schools, holds its interschool swimming sports in a river, placing stronger swimmers in the lanes where the current provides a natural handicap. The association ekes out good money every year to send the form one and two kids on a trip to a big city. One summer they raised over $4000 on a betting tote for parents at the athletic sports.

In an old state house near the Waikura turn-off, on its own in the middle of nowhere, memories of swagmen and Model T Fords are still vibrant and alive in the heart and mind of Sam Taitua. Sam is 70 and a Maori Battalion veteran. For 22 years he was the Potaka roadman—one of 15 employed by local councils to maintain the highway until it was all sealed in 1974. Sam's dad Bob was the Cape Runaway roadman in his time, and for a few years they shared a boundary. 'We'd meet on our horses for a brew by the river, and talk about the vehicles that came through—a few every day,' says Sam.

Sam retired in 1984, but for years afterwards he made a daily patrol of the road out of habit, to clear slips and repair washouts. Today, the Potaka section of 35 averages no more than 200 vehicles a day.

On Hippie Hill, a commune of sorts that has long amused locals by its infighting, I am welcomed by Norm and Glennis Anderson. They live in a solar-powered house on stilts in the treetops, run a wood-fired pottery, and keep a house-cow and a German shepherd called Plato for company. We feast on mountains of baked tofu, spiced vegetables, bean sprouts, yoghurt and dried fruit, and that night I sleep deeply with a hottie and quilts in a bed next to snoring Plato, the thinker.

The commune's 45-ha property was bought in the 1970s by a group of idealists, including one named Jim Jones. Like his namesake's community at Jonestown, the dream fell apart. Some changed their ideals and left. Others argued—over whose patch was whose, stock grazing rights, environmental issues—and then split. Of the present 28 stakeholders, many are gone-address-unknown and not paying their share of rates. 'It's a mess, really,' says Norm. Keeping to yourself, he adds, is the best way to coexist with the dozen other

Pine plantations continue to soak up more and more East Coast country, and change the way of life as farm jobs decline and forestry work increases. Here the chainsaws clearfell a woodlot at Pakira Station in the Waikura Valley.

*The Waikura Valley, halfway between Cape Runaway and Hicks Bay, is the
most isolated farming district in New Zealand, with Te Kumi Station being the
furthest farm by road from any city.*

occupants, each with their own little house in the bush, each with an unofficial subdivision of about a hectare.

'When we came here from Port Waikato,' Glennis says, 'I thought with this being a community it would work really well if you went away for a few days and wanted someone to look after the cow and the chooks. But it doesn't work that way.'

Disillusioned? 'No, not really,' Norm says, 'because we came here in 1988 for our independence and privacy. We were late-starting hippies who took a bit of time to gather some finance and sort out our ideas first. We came here to stay, regardless.'

Big, burly Norm, 42 and 16 stone, has a 10-year-old beard plaited and twisted in dreadlocks, and is on the electoral roll as a Subsistence Peasant. He's never been on the dole, and makes his living as a potter, relieving schoolteacher and part-time forestry worker. He refuses to plant pines, though, saying they are a blot on the landscape. The only part of forestry he likes is the burn-off after the radiata has been harvested.

'I'm a pyromaniac in my heart, which is why I love firing the kiln,' he jokes.

He plays rugby for Hicks Bay—the only Pakeha and the oldest player in the team—and was nicknamed Stormin' Norman for his propping and mauling prowess.

Glennis and I watch Norm in a bruising match against Waiapu, held in the school grounds at Hicks Bay right next to the cemetery. 'Dead ball!' a young girl shrieks when the ball goes over the fence, sending up a roar of laughter from a hundred-odd spectators.

'You're dead now!' taunts a grandmother to the player who goes to fetch it. 'Get the water! Get the water!' bellows Mrs Rangi White, a large woman pacing the sideline. It is the custom to wash away evil spirits with the water, placing it on both the ball and the forehead of the player who retrieves it.

There is plenty more cheek from the sideline, and during a lineout Norm gets into an argument with a woman for telling another player to put the boot in.

'No one really means any harm,' Glennis told me. 'The other day someone called out to an opposition player to give Norman a boot in the backside. "Kick that Pakeha bastard up the arse!" they said. But Rangi White swung round from the sideline and yelled back at them, "You leave our Pakeha bastard alone!"'

Horses are still as valuable in parts of the East Coast as they were at the turn of the century, when bridle trails were the region's main thoroughfares.

6

SUDDENLY EVERYTHING IS DIFFERENT, yet everything the same. It's such a capricious place, this coast. Raw and wild one minute, soft and benevolent the next. From the drowsy hills of the borderlands, the road seeps back to the sea at Cape Runaway, where lagoons of ducks and pukeko float on marshy shores.

From here on to Opotiki the thickly forested ranges of the Raukumaras back almost into the water. A narrow strip—an afterthought of foothills, farms and orchards no more than a few kilometres wide—separates the summits from the sea. Along this ribbon the road runs for 118 km. Sun drums on the blue, blue Bay of Plenty. White Island puffs on the horizon. Wispy waterfalls spill from gullies choked by gnarled pohutukawa. Rocky coves and stony beaches entice the traveller to make stop after stop. And on pastured promontories between river valleys, little villages bask in the glory of it all.

But life is close to the bone everywhere on the East Coast. I pass the weekly tourist bus on its round from Rotorua to Hicks Bay and back: one passenger today. 'Sorry, all credit is cancelled,' declares the blackboard notice at Omaio Store. At another: 'Cigarettes strictly cash—no exceptions—I pay cash and don't even smoke, so why shouldn't you.'

It's an area of marginal television reception, and kids are fond of telling people they get TV1 guaranteed, TV2 if they're lucky and free sky all day long. To send his kids on a school trip, a cannabis grower raffles off a bag of sticky buds among his friends. Old people gather bits of twisted driftwood for pocket money from an Auckland merchant who exports it by the containerload to Korea and Japan for ornamental uses. A contractor's bulldozer is torched because his

Lance Blake, deckhand aboard the cray boat Santa Leah, *empties pots off the* Te Kopua *coastline while skipper Kevin Webb keeps an eye on the job.*

employee set fire to a much-loved puriri tree. I help judge the finals of Te Kaha pub's $1000 karaoke contest, and am warned—quietly in the toilets—to watch out for myself because there are questionable people who will not like the result. People living close to the bone.

From the top of a solitary 3-m rock cone in the middle of the beach at Whangaparaoa, Winston Waititi sweeps an arm across the pretty bay and the tiny Cape Runaway settlement of about 25 families. For more than 30 years he has taught the story of the sacred moki to Cape school children, just as he was taught it by his father. But somehow it doesn't ring true any more, he says, his arm now across his chest. It makes him feel like a hypocrite.

'When I was a kid we could count more than 50 small boats out there, every one of them fishing for moki with hand lines. They were like mosquitoes, none of them moving fast as they had Seagull motors or inboards that used to just putt-putt about the place, and yet they all came back loaded with fish. No one ever felt embarrassed about going down to the beach to pick up a moki,

because there were hundreds of them, and everybody had a right to a feed. Now we get these flash aluminium and fibreglass commercial boats with a couple of hundred horsepower and radars to find the fish—they take everything.'

But Winston is out to stop that. There is no reason, he says, why the iwi can't get the moki stocks back to the olden-day level— 'so long as we can get those damned nets out of it.'

The 55-year-old teacher-principal is an educated, mild-mannered man, and a kaumatua of the Kauaetangohia hapu and marae at the Cape. A stalwart of the East Coast Rugby Union and driving force of the local TVC (Tikirau Victory Club) rugby, netball and tennis club, he also serves as a trustee for various land blocks and as an honorary fisheries officer. He acts as the hapu trust's front man for a call to the Treaty of Waitangi Tribunal and the Ministry of Agriculture and Fisheries to create three taiapure (fisheries) and a protection zone for the moki. The hapu's claim and submission have languished since 1989 with no response from officialdom.

Since the early 1970s, the legendary sacred moki grounds have not produced big catches or attracted hordes of Te Whanau a Apanui for the abundant seasonal harvest, which was controlled tribally and maintained for hundreds of

The reefs around Waihau Bay, on the Bay of Plenty side of East Cape.
Opposite page: Ponga fronds make umbrellas on the beach at Whangaparaoa,
near the Cape, landing place of the waka Tainui and Arawa, which were
guided from the sea by the volcanic plume rising from White Island.

Raukokore's old Catholic church, a stone's throw from the highway, now serves as a carving workshop (see overleaf). A rarity in the mainly Anglican district, the church was built in 1934 to cater for a few local families and Irish roadmen who helped put the road through to Cape Runaway.

years from mid-June to mid-September. The moki have been fished out by commercial set nets in the hands of a few big Gisborne companies and local commercial fishermen. Without basic kai moana supplies, local people have felt hurt—denied their rangatiratanga and unable to stop the destruction of an old resource or act out their responsibility as guardians for future generations.

In Winston's classroom, his ten- to thirteen-year-old pupils have just completed their annual winter project: a study of the moki story and its significance to the hapu. There are moki paintings on the walls, a big mural showing the migratory patterns of the fish, charts in Maori and English listing the rules and rites of moki fishing, and posters welcoming visitors to 'Cape Runaway, home of the sacred moki.'

Across Highway 35 from the 83-year-old school—at the eastern end of Te Whanau a Apanui rohe—Kauaetangohia Marae provides a more stately and definitive record of the moki story because it is intertwined with the ancestral history of the tribe. The original settlers were descendants of the crew of the Tainui canoe which landed here about 1350.

In 1974, gifted Te Whanau a Apanui artists Cliff Whiting and Para Matchitt led a team of students, volunteers and even passing tourists in decorating the interior walls of the wharenui and dining hall with unique tukutuku and kowhaiwhai patterns which depict Kauaetangohia history. The modern graphics of an enormous four-walled mural in the dining hall contain 54 pictures of moki.

'All the Maori of old used to come here every June to catch the moki,' says Winston. 'In the old days it was nothing to be able to count hundreds of moki laid out on the beach when the season was on. We used to go out with our old man, and we were always proud because as kids we hoped our boat would have more than the next one. But it didn't matter who had how many, because there were moki for everybody. I can remember bus loads of our Ngati Porou relations calling in on their way back around the Cape, and everyone would go away with a moki. It was the moki taste that appealed to them—the rich strong flavour.'

Today, though, the moki harvest is merely a memory for older people, and the cause of a grievance among younger people. 'Everyone is running out of patience,' Winston says. 'Of course we're ready to negotiate, but the younger generation are starting to do things like break into commercial chillers where moki are stored. After a few beers, they get quite game and say, "You just give us the word uncle, we'll sort it out."

'These guys have gone through school here, they've learned the rules of the moki and, hello, they realise that what they're told isn't really the case any more. So they get frustrated. When we tell them the reasons for the moki depletion, the situation with quota management and commercial netting, and that we're trying to work through the right channels, they back off. But they won't

Under the direction of master carver Paddy Eruera, carvers Mando Waenga (foreground) and Tiger Waititi apply skills they learned in jail to the restoration of Hine Mahuru, the meeting house of Raukokere's Wairuru Marae.

Home late from a fishing trip at Waihau Bay.

'Please don't disturb our penguins nesting under the church,' says a sign at the entrance to historic Christ Church at Raukokore. The door is always open. The beautifully restored interior (opposite page), within this fine example of gothic architecture, is credited to a settler named Duncan Stirling, who designed and built it without any knowledge of architecture in 1896.

wait for ever. We're just wondering why the hang we're not getting anywhere.'

To the locals, it's no surprise that the moki have all but disappeared from the waters of Cape Runaway or, to be precise, Taungawaka, a rocky bay nearby where the first fleet made its epic landfall. In the traditions of the Kauaetangohia it is taught that if ever the moki is ill-treated, it will return for ever to the waters of Hawaiki from whence the moki people also came.

Some people don't understand local concern, Winston says, because to many the moki is just a fish to use as bait in a craypot—not a delicacy to be sought after when it is fat for a few winter months. Its head is sacred, not to be abused by netting or striking. 'Even the custom of protecting the head makes sense to us because there is no kick in a moki when it has been lured up on a hook. There's no need to strike it dead. A secret to eating the moki is that there is green bile in it which makes the body sour unless it is drained out of the mouth, by hanging the fish by its tail. You see, this is more than just a story.'

Questions the authorities cannot or will not answer are why the moki have gone from Cape Runaway, why tribal submissions for fishery protection have fallen on deaf ears and when, if ever, they will take action. Part of the explanation is that moki aren't an important species: ninth most common finfish caught commercially in New Zealand, almost all of it between Bay of Plenty and Kaikoura, with 404 tonnes caught in 1993–94, and a peak total of 960 tonnes caught in 1970 and 1979. Adult moki migrate from Kaikoura in late April and May to spawn until September between Mahia Peninsula and East Cape, then disappear. According to MAF scientists, the moki return 'south towards Kaikoura', but according to the

lore of the moki people at Cape Runaway, that's when they go home to Hawaiki.

Treaty of Waitangi Tribunal spokesperson Vanessa Byrnes gives no hope of a hearing for years, possibly. 'I do sympathise with the Cape Runaway people,' she says. 'I agree it is a bloody shame people have to wait so long, but the Treaty business is now an industry, and people are just jumping on the bandwagon.'

AN HOUR OR SO DOWN the road at Te Kaha, Jacko Parata says he was 'too staunch' about Maori fishing rights when he landed the job of fishing operations manager for Te Runanga o Whanau a Apanui, the tribal authority, in 1990.

Today he's in charge of a live crayfishing unit that handles and exports mainly to Japan about 25 tonnes a year, two commercial fishing boats, tribal quota management, a training programme for young local men, the iwi's equity investment in public company Moana Pacific Fisheries Ltd, and plans for an offshore mussel farm near Te Kaha.

'I had to do some internal gear changes when I first got the job,' says the 42-year-old, who joined the runanga to co-ordinate an iwi research and development planning MACCESS scheme in 1988. Before that, Tiaki Rangikawanoa Parata, born and bred at Te Kaha and schooled at Hamilton Boys High School, had been a jack-of-all-trades: labourer, encyclopedia salesman, butcher, barman and school caretaker. Jacko and his wife Ethel have 4 children aged 12 to 18, and as a family have always fished in the idyllic waters of the East Coast rohe.

Now Jacko champions the runanga's expanding fishing operation, and believes its value as a cash contributor and a community business employing about ten people is now well accepted despite early scepticism and criticism. 'I

used to think no one had the right to sell our crayfish, but when the runanga asked me to manage their new live crayfishing operation, I had to do a bit of soul searching. I was too staunch.'

He attributes the commercial success and growth of the fishing business to sound strategic planning by the runanga, an early commitment to learning about the fishing industry, a long-running relationship with Moana Pacific Fisheries, and the leadership of runanga boss Riki Gage, 38, a former university lecturer who came home to lead the runanga in its fisheries development plan. Five years ago the runanga became a foundation Te Kupenga investor in Moana Pacific, and at the same time purchased a training boat and crayfish quota under a Mana Enterprise Scheme. With temporary holding tanks and facilities loaned by Moana Pacific, it set up the live crayfish export operation. All told the runanga committed itself to about $500,000 of investment.

Looking back, Jacko says the early research work proved to him that maatauranga (information/education) is a prerequisite to any iwi business programme. 'You've got to have the knowledge first, then you can set up the infrastructure.' With the crayfishing operation, the runanga purchased 7.5 tonnes of quota and leveraged another 17.5 tonnes by inviting local fishermen to form

Whanarua Bay banana grower and nurseryman Hoani Park (opposite page) is a merchant and trader who uses his Wanganui Collegiate education to hustle the Auckland markets for a living from his idyllic retreat at Whanarua Bay (above).

supply contracts with it. They were led by Waihau Bay fisherman Romio Kemara, a member of the 28th Maori Battalion, whose attitude was that 'he'd fish for us if it was for the benefit of the iwi.'

Now the operation employs two to three permanent staff and occupies five or six privately owned cray boats. With annual turnover of more than $800,000 and a brand new live cray plant purpose built on runanga land at Te Kaha, the fishermen get an average yield of about $30 a kilogram, which is the main reason there are no longer any roadside sales of crayfish in Te Whanau a Apanui rohe. It's a price the local market could never match.

The runanga's two commercial fishing boats are based in Tauranga, where Te Whanau a Apanui fisherman Willie Walker and his wife Carol—who privately operate three boats of their own—function as 'de facto managers' of the two iwi boats. Says Jacko, 'Last week when I was up there Willie and Carol and their daughter Maraea were all down at the slipway helping paint one of our boats. We tie up together in port, and they keep an eye on everything for us. Their support and advice is like family and it's one of the big factors in favour of the iwi fishing operation.'

The runanga's latest project is in aquaculture and will soon see commercial mussel farms established at Little Awanui, the sheltered waters inside Motunui Island near Te Kaha. Jacko has high hopes for the farm based on an apparent niche opportunity identified nearly ten years ago by a former fisheries officer who was associated with a Japanese eel-farming venture at Te Kaha in the 1970s and who stayed on when the farm closed to continue research into aquaculture. 'We plan to do further trials on the growth rate of mussels here, but we think we may have a spat season which is out of sync with the rest of the industry. This could well give us a niche opportunity to supply spat or seed mussels to other farms.'

'Our people are very supportive of the fishing operation,' says Jacko, 'because they can see the progress we have made. It's also kai for everyone. Often for tangis and iwi functions we are able to supply kai moana from our own operation or from Moana Pacific. That's when people can see the real value of this business. It enhances tribal mana when you can manuhiri in the traditional way.'

ON 35 I'M A PANTHEIST in paradise. At Waihau Bay I spy a 17-kg 'runaway red' snapper in Bill Hol's freezer, then catch my own share of bounty from the sea: in two hours we have a surfeit of hapuka, snapper, terakihi, gurnard and 'lesser' species. On the mighty Motu River I raft and canoe a virgin wilderness where time and eternity at last do meet. On the northern flanks of the Raukumara Range I ride with Te Puna Frontier, a horsetrekking outfit run by Red Duigan and Grim Stanbridge, listening to them talk of the 80 wild boars

Maize cropping forms part of an income for many East Coast landowners.
Opposite page: Highway 35 at Te Kaha.

Previous page: Pohutukawa, tapestried by wind and weather, pervade the
temperate Bay of Plenty coastline from Te Araroa to Opotiki and beyond.

and 30 sows they hunted down with dogs and knives last year.

The Coast is so provident, so rich in game and fish and fruit and vegetables, that reasonably able folks can live quite well off the land itself. This produces a cavalier attitude toward cash: money is best spent on toys, travel and luxury items. The produce of the land is traded for goods and services—mutton or beef for pork, crayfish for wetfish, cows for horses, labour for timber, firewood, car parts or plumbing, roading metal for driveways, fenceposts, and so on.

At 6 a.m. over cups of tea in front of the wood-fired coal range of a busy kitchen, I sit with a crayfishing family who are planning out their day's work while the sun comes up. Dave de Mant, 67, tough and gruff in a prickly woollen singlet, jeans and gumboots, turns two loaves of bread and a leg of cold mutton into sandwiches for the fishermen, his son Tangaroa and crewman Ashley White. Outside a tractor motor purrs for half an hour while we get ready, warming up before Dave, supposedly retired after nearly 50 years at sea, launches Tangaroa's 9-m boat by 4-wheel-driving through a maze of debris at daybreak.

To clear a path through the night's 2-m-high stack of driftwood, Dave bulldozes logs and seaweed with the tractor, then backs its trailer and vessel into the surging sea. Tangaroa guns the big Volvo engine of *Miss Molly*, named after his Maori mother, and we pull out to haul pots for the morning. Dave will wait at home with Molly and Tangaroa's wife Vicky and his grandchildren, repairing pots and gear, listening to the marine radio and calling the boat for 'just checking' conversations.

From the verge of the water the land rises uniformly, with green and sloping declivities, until from gently rolling hillsides and moderate elevations it insensibly swells into the lofty and majestic heights of the Raukumaras. The beautiful aspect of the rocky shoreline is heightened by overhanging pohutukawa and nikau palms. This rugged, broken strip of coast between Raukokore and Te Kaha is arguably the most spectacular piece of the entire East Cape region. Today the crisp morning sky is strafed with yellow and pink cloud which will burn off in a few hours. The wind is chill but the work is warm, and the fishermen are in their element. Scores of pots are lifted, and scores of crays are caught for fresh export to Japan.

'See that dark bit,' says Tangaroa, pointing me in the direction of an escarpment dripping with greenery 100 m from where we are fishing. 'It's very tapu, that place. We never catch crays there. I never put pots down there." Tangaroa explains that olden-day warriors used to kill and eat their enemy captives here. It was a kainga, or place of shelter for travelling tribesmen returning from battles further afield. There is superstition attached to the site nowadays, and only a fool would ignore it, he says.

After four hours of non-stop pot pulling, Tangaroa returns me to the shore

Fishing is a way of life on the Coast's sheltered Bay of Plenty side. When guests are coming, Merlyn Craw, a retired commercial crayfisherman, likes to head down to the beach near Te Kaha to put out a few pots.

The sinking sun glances off the horizon behind a curve in the final stretch of the 110 km-long Motu River.

Previous pages: The Motu, the biggest river on the East Coast, has gouged out a braid of channels where it reaches the ocean beneath Highway 35.

by nosing *Miss Molly* on to a reef out from his home. I jump, holding my camera and a koha of three huge crays in a plastic bag above my head. I get wet to my waist and my gumboots fill with water. Stumbling and gasping from the cold shock, to the laughter of the two fishermen, I hear a gravelly voice on the shore.

'Get a bit wet, boy!' Dave calls. 'Come on up to the house and have a cuppa. We'll soon warm you up.' In the kitchen again, as a puddle of salt water forms on the floor under my seat, Molly rebukes Dave for monopolising the conversation with me. 'You be quiet, Dave de Mant,' she tells him, adding an order I often heard in households on this journalistic journey: 'Don't keep our visitor all to yourself.'

Molly's late father Romana Ratima was a prestigious elder and speaker from Whakatane's Ngatiawa hapu, and her mother was from the local Whakatohea tribe. Fishing has been a way of life in her family for more generations than she can remember. It was divine fate that brought her and Dave, an immigrant English sailor, together in the 1950s, she says. Even the name of their son Tangaroa, which means god of the sea, was divinely appointed, albeit a choice in which she had no say at the time.

In 1962, Dave and his fishing mate Joey Haia had the bad luck of losing their 6-m open boat while fishing in heavy seas near Whale Island, off Whakatane. Stranded on the island for six days in stormy weather with little but their fishing lines and two half-gallon flagons of beer, they camped on Ngawha Beach, where hot sulphuric water comes up through the sand, and fished with lures from the rocks for food. Everyone thought they had perished. On the sixth day, however, they attracted the attention of a passing boat and got a ride back to Whakatane. Of course there were jubilant phone calls and family reunions. Says Dave: 'At the time Molly and I had been trying for a second child, and Molly was pregnant, so we decided to name our child Tangaroa after the god of the sea who brought us back from the sea.'

'No we didn't!' Molly objected. 'I had no choice in it—*you* chose his name and the first I knew of it was when I read the birth notice *you* put in the newspaper.' There was no malice in this disagreement, though. 'We already had a daughter, and we wanted a son to keep the tradition of fishing alive in the family,' Molly said. 'And Tangaroa has taken over from Dave so beautifully. Dave is supposed to be retired, but he just keeps tagging along, don't you, Dave!'

At Whanarua Bay, the most gorgeous of all the bays on this highway, I wander unbelievingly among groves of macadamias, bananas, pineapples and nikau palms as I search out a hidden place of the past—a holy headland pockmarked with caves and archways. From a vantage point on the roadside overlooking the gnarled headland called Motu-a-ruhe, or island of fern, I let the afternoon sun bake away the vague, sad sense of longing that always descends on

The highway sweeps inland after tracing a parallel path with driftwood-laden Hawai Beach.

me at Whanarua. I always yearn to stay for ever. The gentle beauty of the place suits my mood. The hills, alive with subtropical luxuriance, spill down toward the sea in waves of variegated green. The sound of the surf rises faintly from the bay below and mingles with the lazy hum of insects, the sigh of the breeze in the trees and a symphony of birdsong studded by the calls of bellbirds and tuis. Below, a series of jagged rock spires too steep to carry vegetation rise like sentinels just above the bay. They might have been parapets of some alien civilisation.

The kaitiaki or guardian of this place might also be from another world, except that his tipuna or ancestors have always possessed Motu-a-ruhe. Hoani Park inherited part of it, and leases the rest from family. His 22-acre property supports nearly 600 macadamia trees, about 250 clumps of banana plants up to 4 m high, a pineapple grove, a shelter-belt cypress nursery and a huge nikau nursery of around 10,000 palms. The nikau are spread through the property—older palms clustered in natural clearings beneath mature native bush, younger plants bedded in rich humus plots set into the dark forest underfloor.

Hoani also runs a portable sawmill to handle windfallen giants from the East Coast bush-country and native timber logs which he salvages when they come down rivers in storms and end up on beaches. One day he would like to build cottages among his plantations for renting to visitors, and an amphitheatre stage for performing arts and concerts.

Hoani, 52, but as alert and energetic as a man 20 years younger, is unusually well educated and well spoken for a Coastie—the result of a secondary education at Wanganui Collegiate, where he had the distinction of being the only East Coast Maori.

'I hated it, basically,' he says of his Collegiate experience. He was forced to go there, as was his father, who later studied horticulture at university before returning to the coast as a teacher and horticultural adviser. For four years Hoani begged his parents to let him come home from Wanganui to escape one of the poshest private schools in the country. 'Wanganui Collegiate put me off school for ever,' he says. 'I was a fish out of water, and I pined for my home on the Coast all the time. I missed the beaches and the bush, the fishing and the hunting. It just wasn't the right environment for me.' He got his way in the end; his father arranged a job for him as a farmhand in the isolated Waikura Valley. He has worked the land for a living ever since.

For four years while his cavendish banana plantation got established, he was a wharfie at Mt Maunganui and commuted home at weekends. To make a living gardening and trading produce, he used to drive Highway 35 round to Tikitiki and Ruatoria every week vending fruit and vegetables but the advent of Eftpos and its cashless society killed the business. Nowadays he trades mainly in Auckland. He and Maria, his wife, have 6 children aged 24 to 29 and living

away from the Coast. They share the family home with Hoani's elderly mother and an ever-changing number of mokopuna. Tending the exotic garden and plantations in the subtropical microclimate of Whanarua Bay is a whanau responsibility—and judging by its fruitfulness and neatness, a shared pleasure—but Hoani is the bright-eyed, smooth-talking entrepreneur who turns it into dosh.

Once or twice a month he takes a truck load of produce to Auckland to hustle the weekend flea markets or knock on doors until he meets his income target of $1000 per trip. A typical load might be 100 kg of ripe bananas, 20 or 30 potted nikaus, 50 to 100 pieces of ornamental driftwood which fetch a few dollars each, rocks for gardens, banana flowers and leaves which are keenly sought after by Thai restaurants, arga seaweed and sometimes crayfish to raffle in South Auckland pubs. 'Anything that can make a dollar will go on the truck,' Hoani says. 'Anything goes in this business. Even if I'm left with a pile of useless looking rocks and driftwood I can get rid of them by stopping at the garden centres along Great South Road and selling them in a cheap bulk deal. I never go home without selling out.'

Back in the Whanarua Bay time warp, fantails fluttering peacefully about my head, two hollow arches shaped like cathedral doors are the obvious point of entry to the caves at the foot of the Park family land. The climb down through the bush past Hoani's nikau plots and double-overhead banana plants is like walking in a Garden of Eden. I step through the doors to a scene that bombards the senses, numbing the mind with its intense beauty. The headland is surrounded by several tiny rock islands that rob the sea of its force and send frothy foam into shore. A terrace no more than 5 m wide provides a natural landing in front of the caves. Two natural bathing pools linked to spring water sit at the cave entrance. A narrow channel on one side makes the landing seem like an island, as the sea rushes past and wraps around and behind the headland. It pours into another bay of equal virginal beauty, 40 m wide with dense native bush to the sea's edge. The cave itself is an L-shaped room perhaps 10 m long with a gable ceiling. A chunky carved wooden table and seat at the entrance faces out to sea like an altar. There are two old bed bases, fireplaces and charcoal drawings on the walls. I understand why they call it Te Ano Whakairo (the cave of writing), and it inspires me.

Many times since I have visited this hallowed room of rock and dreamed back into the past when travellers would stop here to rest and write. The first pilgrims to this Coast inscribed messages from their journeys: who they were, where they were headed, when they passed this way. When the Pakeha first came to live here, sailing ships would call and leave freight and supplies in the cave for settlers. I leave my mark, too. It's a child's simple prayer of thanks. For the Coast. For the road. My road.

From Opotiki's Tablelands, layer upon layer of hill and mountain run off into the distant Raukumara Range.

Previous pages: Harvest time beneath kiwifruit vines in Opotiki's horticultural district.

Opotiki's biennial Fibre & Fleece Festival draws designs in natural fibres from all round the country for three days in April. The festival culminates in a fashion show and awards night, an East Coast social occasion typical for its unsophisticated, uncontrived proceedings.

For $2 the Opotiki Museum will let you wander for hours among rooms and
buildings full of artefacts and heirlooms, tractors and buggies, cash registers
and telephone exchanges, all gifted by local residents. The Opotiki Heritage
and Agricultural Society is a voluntary organisation with one of the largest
collections of colonial memorabilia in New Zealand.
Opposite page: Daybreak arrives over the Opotiki district in the north-western
corner of the Cape. With a population of 4500, it is the second-largest
community on the coast, after Gisborne.

Opotiki storekeeper George Shalfoon's family have run the general store and hardware business since 1895. George himself started work for the family as an itinerant hawker in 1936, travelling the coast road with clothing, hardware and produce. His 1938 Ford V8 pickup served as a delivery vehicle until the motor died a few years ago, but he could not bear to part with the vehicle. It will stay in the shop's rear store.

Following pages: a finger of land pointing toward the rising sun: East Cape, place of first light.

ACKNOWLEDGEMENTS

The authors gratefully acknowledge all who have helped to make possible the publication of this book — part travelogue, part documentary — particularly the individuals and organisations named, portrayed or quoted, and our families who showed great patience during our absences while gathering material.

Special thanks go to Kennedy Warne, editor of *New Zealand Geographic*, for inspiration, encouragement and incisive editing. We are grateful for the friendship and hospitality of many East Coast people, particularly Don and Louia Blakeney of Anaura Bay, Nig Manuel of Rangitukia, Grim and Vanessa Stanbridge and Red and Tui Duigan of Te Puna Frontier at Hicks Bay, the Rastafarian community around Ruatoria, the Waipiro Bay Marae Committee, and Ken Barsdell and Cammy Savage of Kutarere.

For support services we thank Kodak (NZ) Ltd and Graham Bell of Bell-Air Whakatane.

Research and travel costs for this book were jointly subsidised by: